DELTA TEACHER DEVELOPMENT SERIES

Series editors Mike Burghall and Lindsay Clandfield

Culture in our Classrooms

Teaching language through cultural content

Gill Johnson and Mario Rinvolucri

Published by
DELTA PUBLISHING
Quince Cottage
Hoe Lane
Peaslake
Surrey GU5 9SW
England

www.deltapublishing.co.uk

First published 2010

ISBN 978-1-905085-21-7

Edited by Mike Burghall
Designed by Christine Cox
Cover photo © iStockphoto.com/Ilya Terentyev
Printed by Halstan & Co., Amersham, Bucks, England

From the authors

I grew up in England, the daughter of a northern Protestant patriarch and a southern Jewish matriarch. Both my parents believed they were right and wronged. My mother was totally unprepared for life in a northern community where men were 'the rulers' of their households. My father was equally unprepared for life with a woman expecting to rule her own. As a child, of course I knew my parents were not the same as those of my neighbours. I had a different accent from my friends and my brothers were both very talented musicians who practised their instruments each evening. This marked us out as different, too.

As a child I was struck by how different the families of my parents were. My mother's family was a huge crowd of noisy, argumentative members. My father's family was much more closed and I never really knew what they were thinking. I can remember wondering which family I really belonged to and switched my allegiances often.

I used to visit the homes of my Indian and Pakistani friends, play games and sample their fabulous homemade sweets, cakes and drinks after school. Their houses seemed really exotic, with the shrines and incense of the Hindu homes, the Spartan elegance of the Muslim households and the beautiful, colourful, perfumed saris worn by the women. Gradually, the Asian families started to move away and into their own language/religion-based communities where it was more difficult to visit them. People looked at me strangely: a white girl walking about in 'their' territory. It became increasingly obvious that I was not welcome.

My friends were equally divided. The Muslims who were friendly with Hindus at school didn't mix with them at home, while some of the class were against people who mixed with different ethnic groups and were hostile towards those of us who did. I railed against all these groups who wouldn't just 'get on with it' together. I remember my mother telling me that there would always be prejudice and that nothing would ever change: it had been the same for her when she was a child. She had quickly decided she didn't want to be Jewish. I was shocked to learn that she had been frightened into wanting to be other than herself. I'd thought my mum wasn't afraid of anything.

It is this belonging and not belonging, understanding and misunderstanding, wanting to be 'myself' and learning that my 'self' was sometimes a separate thing from the identity given me by others, that gave birth to the questions and ideas that, over the years, have become this book.

Gill

I was brought up in a little village in North Wales until the age of 13. The languages of the home were English and Italian. My father was an Italian immigrant, my mother was half English, half German. None of us spoke Welsh, the language we heard all around us.

Acutely culturally unaware, I took the volcanic cultural events of my childhood to be simply what was meant to happen, what did happen, and I had no thinking tools at that time for analysis. Edward Hall, Hofstede and Trompenaars had yet to write their seminal books! It is with analytical hindsight that I now understand the huge part that cultural misunderstanding and conflict have played in my life, both in my home of origin and later.

My father would regularly fly off the handle. My mother would withdraw into her shell. One a doctor of engineering and the other with her PhD in comparative literature, Daniel Goleman might say that they lacked emotional intelligence, while Howard Gardner might refer to lack of interpersonal intelligence. My feeling is that it was *cultural* awareness that they lacked.

At 13, I was dispatched to spend five years in an English 'public school' as a boarder. The place was a 'total' society in that, like a naval ship or a prison, it claimed to control every aspect of life. At home, I had developed the ability to be on my own: clock-time had never seemed very important. At school, everything was measured to the minute. Those years severely imprinted me with values that I now consciously reject but which, I fear, wander freely inside me.

The transposition into a new family is probably one of the most universal areas of culture shock we experience. Upon marriage, I 'immigrated' into an upper-middle-class Anglo-French family. Entering this family was deeply confusing, in terms of not perceiving or understanding the web of tacit assumptions and presuppositions they lived by. They were kind, well-intentioned and supportive and therefore I could not understand the uncanny distance I felt between them and me. And I guess they, too, will have had problems in dealing with this intimate intruder.

Much of the above has always been present in my mind, but it is the writing of this book that has drawn these matters into sharp focus. How I could have spent so many years as an EFL teacher without focusing on culture in a conscious way is a matter of wonderment to me. The writing of *Culture in our Classrooms* with Gill has added a thrilling new dimension to my passionate enjoyment of teaching.

Mario

Contents

Contents

Foreword

As language students study, or prepare to study, work and live on the global stage, they need to understand how people *in* and *from* other societies operate, how to get on with them and see things from 'the other' point of view as well as their own. This places the understanding of culture at the centre of the language curriculum, as opposed to a marginal option on the fringe of classroom activity. However, one problem is that many teachers do not fully understand how culture relates to the process of language learning. There is a huge need to achieve a re-orientation by defining clearly and painlessly the role of culture in our classrooms.

Building rapport and credibility successfully with people from other societies demands interpersonal skills of listening actively, observing behaviour and appreciating their values and expectations. It is an emotional, affective – and not just intellectual – process and, in many ways, the study of culture fits into the domain of 'emotional intelligence' as defined by Daniel Goleman.

Traditionally, 'culture' has been seen as an explanation of 'civilisation' or 'life and institutions' of the country whose language is being taught. Of course, there is a place for this knowledge transfer and a need for interactive activity to achieve this, focusing on attitudes and values, institutions and behaviour. But in the long run, and maybe more important, is the learning of 'culture skills': ideas and techniques that help students to adapt and fit into new environments, whether on study tours, school trips – or studying and working, both at home and abroad.

Most important, however, is *attitude* to the teaching of culture. To be successful, any cultural interchange must be two-way – my experience of *you* changes *me*, and vice versa. In the process, all of us become more internationally-minded, at the same time learning to appreciate our own roots through comparison with other societies. Cultural studies should emphasise our common humanity, while studying the different routes we follow to achieve it. It is laudable that Gill Johnson and Mario Rinvolucri, by inserting their own very personal stories, bring out the principle of inter-culturality so strongly. Perhaps that is this book's most important message.

Barry Tomalin
International House, London

In offering our cultural perspectives, and 'indulging' in some initial autobiographical material, we align ourselves with the humanistic anthropological tradition which claims that no observation can be neutral or 'objective', and that the reader has therefore a right to know the forces playing on the minds of the observers. In going through the text and experimenting with the activities, you will correct our biases – in your own biased way!

The authors

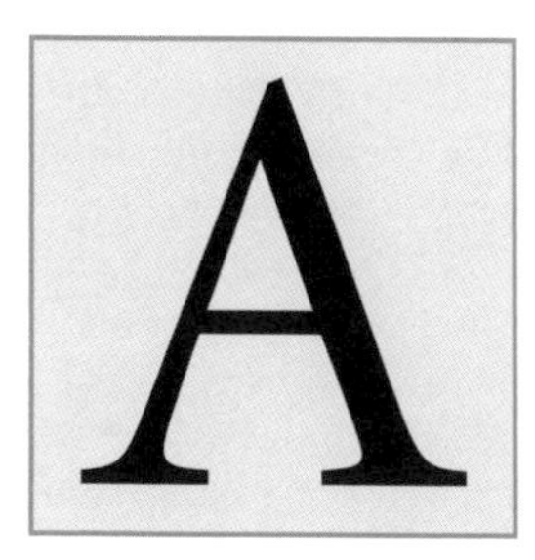

Culture in our classrooms

We can't get away from it. As we shall see, culture is everywhere. It is in the writing of these pages and, inevitably, in what takes place in our classrooms, affecting all aspects of our teaching and our students' learning. It is:

- *here* (where we are) and *there* (where we aren't);
- *up* (what we might aspire to) and *down* (what we might despise);
- *high* (what we revere) and *low* (what we nevertheless enjoy);
- *in* (where we belong) and *out* (where we don't).

A number of classroom activities from Part B are cross-referenced below and throughout Part A as they may add a further perspective to our points as we make them.

There are widely differing, even conflicting, views within historical and current thought on the notion of culture and, in this brief account, it will be for each of us to decide what fits with our own way of thinking. The word 'culture' itself comes from the Italian *cultura*, stemming from *colere*, which means 'to cultivate'. Its etymology would support the notion, therefore, that culture is a shifting, changing, moving thing, that grows through a society as it progresses.

Culture and current thinking

Definitions and explanations of culture come to us from two major areas of thinking. The first area for consideration is that of the humanities, where *'it focuses on the way a social group represents itself and others through its material productions, be they works of art, literature, social institutions or artifacts of everyday life, and the mechanisms for their reproduction and preservation through history'.*[1]

What strikes you in a strange culture?
Page 72

Claire Kramsch, whose words these are, is here talking about the things which strike us when we visit a foreign place for the first time: for example, clothes, money, architecture, cooking utensils, etc. It is often the case that the casual tourist will never go beyond these first impressions. It is also the case that visitors to the culture may use these artifacts to make judgements, sometimes negative ones, about the culture they represent.

The second area is that of the social sciences, where *'it refers to what educators like Howard Nostrand call the "ground of meaning", ie the attitudes and beliefs, ways of thinking, behaving and remembering shared by members of that community'.*[2] Nostrand is referring to the hidden patterns, the hidden rules of belief and behaviour that govern everyday living, and this is one of the main areas which is explored in social anthropology. Howard Nostrand was an American linguist and francophile, who believed passionately in cross-cultural awareness and spent his life trying to foster better communication between nations. He died in 2004.

Beliefs behind behaviours
Page 26

A principal aim of *Culture in our Classrooms* is to offer practical activities to help our students understand these secret patternings and better interpret them.

Culture and society

Culture is *'man's medium; there is not one aspect of human life that is not touched and altered by culture.[...] It is the least studied aspects of culture that influence behavior in the deepest and most subtle ways.'* [3]

This quote from Edward T Hall, perhaps the grandfather of Western cultural studies, illustrates what we, the authors, firmly believe to be true: some of the deepest, strongest beliefs and patterns of behaviour emerge from the minutiae of everyday life. A simple example taken from Hall's work is that of 'time'. One assumes that everyone knows what time is, and yet in different parts of the world it is clearly perceived very differently, as is evident in the varied behaviours relating to this concept. Hall makes the distinction between monochronic and polychronic understanding of time. In a monochronic culture, it is assumed that a person doing a task cannot be disturbed. They must do one thing at a time. At a Japanese reception desk in a hotel, guests must wait their turn. In a polychronic culture it is acceptable for a person to multi-task: at a Brazilian reception desk, it is perfectly alright for a client not currently being dealt with to ask the receptionist a quick question. Another way of looking at time is simply to ask yourself what 'being late' or 'being on time' means in your own country and in some others that you have been to.

Time is of the essence
Page 61

Talking and turn taking
Page 60

'Culture refers to widely shared ideals, values, formation and uses of categories, assumptions about life and goal-directed activities that become unconsciously or subconsciously accepted as 'right' and 'correct' by people who identify themselves as members of a society.' [4]

In the above quote from Richard Brislin, we have picked out 'categories' and 'assumptions', as these are much harder to pinpoint and therefore perhaps more interesting than ideals and values, which are generally much easier to identify.

Cultural categorisations
Page 21

Images in difference cultures
Page 27

- **Categories** affect the way we look at a whole area of culture. In Western music, for example, we tend to use 4/4 rhythm and major keys as a standard. However, Eastern European music may not use 4/4 and tends to use minor keys. In Western music, we use minor keys to invoke melancholy or sadness. Eastern European composers may not even consider this when using a minor key. Categories govern our thought all the more powerfully precisely because they are taken for granted.
- **Assumptions** are sometimes deeply buried, although they do surface in proverbs. An example might be the English proverb *The early bird catches the worm*. The assumption here, in the UK, is that it is good to 'do': to be pro-active and energetic in one's life and work. These qualities are perceived as deserving of reward. This assumption is paralleled by the assumption in UK schools that the first part of the morning is prime study time: *'Culture is always linked to moral values, notions of good and bad, right and wrong, beautiful and ugly'*. [5]

Because moral values are so deeply embedded within a person, people may feel the need to defend them when encountering another set in another society. This is an area that can cause bitter conflict between cultures.

Culture and the individual

The problem with all of this is that there is no attempt to merge what is idiosyncratic with what is culturally consensually accepted by the society within which the individual lives.

Note the difference
Page 46

Maybe linguistics can help us. Let us take 'Juan', who generally speaks standard Castilian Spanish. Because Juan is 25, he will often use expressions current among people of the same gender in this age group across the middle class in Spanish cities. Some of the things he says have a tinge of the dialect of the town where he lives, Valladolid. Juan comes from a large family and he speaks in ways similar to his siblings and cousins: this is his *famililect*. Some aspects of his speech are completely his own, and cannot be accounted for by age or gender, dialect or 'famililect'. This aspect of Juan's speech is his *idiolect*.

This linguistic scheme may be usefully transposed to things in the cultural area. Juan sees the world with Spanish eyes, and his beliefs and values are Spanish. His 'ground of meaning' is shared with other members of this culture. If you move closer to Juan, you find that his assumptions and attitudes are similar to other Spanish people of his class, age and gender. Move in closer still, and you will find the culture that Juan shares most intimately is that of his family. In the same way that Juan has his own idiosyncratic way of speaking Spanish, his 'idiolect', so he will have his own unique take on the beliefs of the various cultural groups he belongs to. He will have his own 'idioculture', which will partly contrast with the general culture he belongs to.

Groups I belong to
Page 28

Culture and values

Culture is responsible for the way we make sense of the world. It gives us the rules, laws and mores that guide us through our lives inside our societies. Within the comfort zones of our societies, our cultures have made us feel safe because we know exactly what is expected of us and how we should behave in any given situation, so we can predict, with some accuracy, how things will be. We also know what sanctions are available (for both law and rule breakers) for those who do not behave in accordance with our cultural norms and values. Growing up in a society, we internalise these rules, etc, and they become the 'natural' way of things, so far as we are concerned. However, this 'natural order' can be strongly challenged when we step into another culture and experience a different 'natural order' which we may find simply different or even deeply shocking. We may judge, harshly, these societies which do not conform to our own expectations of 'normal behaviour' and 'acceptable opinions'.

Rules for life
Page 38

Mario:
When I first went to India, I was non-plussed not to be thanked for the present I brought my hosts. What I hoped would have delighted them, a Russian tablecloth, was simply taken and put to one side. Nothing was said. I did not know what to think and felt both confused and let down. The convention in UK culture is for the recipient of a gift to say nice things about it and to proffer thanks. The convention in India is to make no fuss at all about a gift, the belief in this culture being that it is unseemly to make a 'song and dance' about a gift, as to do so would be to not take the gift giver's generosity for granted.

Once you read a clinical explanation like the above for difference in cultural behaviour, it seems so simple, and yet bare intellectual understanding does not, at once, dissipate the negative emotion, the culture shock that gurgles through you.

A lesson I learned
Page 40

Geert Hofstede, in *Cultures and Organizations* [6], calls culture 'the software of the mind'. His metaphor describes the enormous effect of culture on our everyday lives. He believes that although we all have what he calls 'human nature' and genetic heritage from our families, by far the greatest factor influencing our everyday behaviour is culture.

Icebergs
Page 58

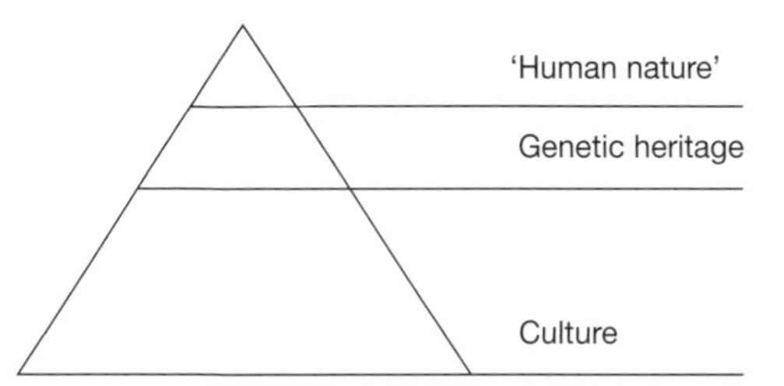

Fons Trompenaars, in his book *Riding the Waves of Culture* [7], uses the image of an onion to describe culture. The core beliefs of any given society are at the centre of the onion and from these are formed many 'layers', like laws, religion, rituals, education systems, etc. The 'outer skin' of the onion represents aspects of the culture that can be seen by outsiders, like

Onion ring culture
Page 53

buildings, transport, money and clothes, all of which could be described as 'products' of a culture. Although the products inevitably change over time, they will reflect the beliefs of the society to which they belong.

Onion ring diagram (adapted from Trompenaars' model)

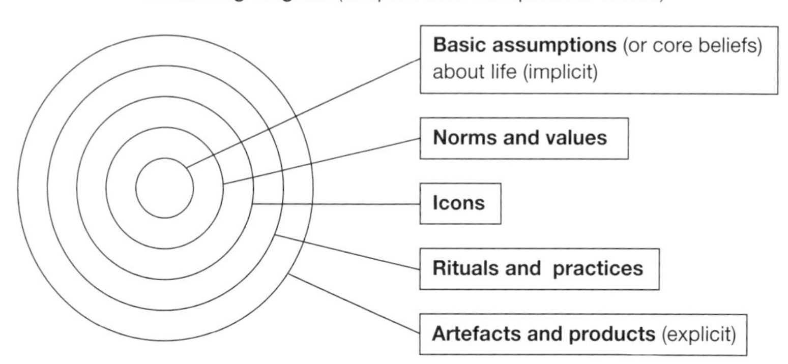

Culture words
Page 57

Trompenaars and Hofstede have been roundly criticised in the English Language Teaching world lately for their views, which are considered essentialist in nature. Essentialist thinking perceives the difference between cultures to be key, thus creating and upholding stereotypes and maintaining an 'us versus them' standpoint. However, we think there is much merit in the above metaphors. They have greatly helped us in that they provided a useful framework from which to start thinking about culture. Although there is doubtless huge diversity within any local culture, we do believe that there are still recognisable patterns of behaviour associated with a particular region, whether or not everyone in that region chooses to abide by the pattern.

We and they
Page 68

Culture and behaviour

Everyone living within any home culture, be it regional or national, at some level will instinctively see the difference between what *is* and what *is not* acceptable behaviour in any given context. We are reminded here of the anthropologist Kate Fox, in the preface to her book *Watching the English* [8], admitting some nervousness before conducting an experiment into English people's reactions to 'queue jumping', as her hypothesis was that the reactions were likely to be very negative.

Queue jumping means to join a queue surreptitiously, near or at the front, rather than at the back, as is normal in the UK. For the majority of English people, this practice is tantamount to a 'deadly sin'. Although others in the queue may be furious with the queue jumper, they tend not to chastise the sinner with more than a sigh, a 'tut tut' or the raising of an eyebrow, because open confrontation is difficult for many English people. However, queue jumpers will be given to understand that they have sinned. People in the queue may talk together about the rudeness of the queue jumpers or give them meaningful admonishing looks. The poor sinners may not even be aware there is a queue they should be in. Kate Fox knew, before beginning her experiment, that she would be, at best, an object of reproach and, at worst, of hatred. If this all sounds extreme or even trivial, ask yourself how you feel when someone contravenes an important behaviour rule in your culture.

Four ways of complaining
Page 81

Given that cultural norms provide us with comfort and stability, if we are confronted with manifestations that challenge these norms, we may react quite fiercely. Often the shock we suffer (based entirely on our own norms) leads to negative judgement and, without communication between the two sides, opinions can become entrenched and conflict can occur.

This is my life!
Page 55

A female immigrant coming to the UK from, say, Afghanistan, could be appalled at the 'immodest' way in which UK women dress. She may, without any dialogue on the subject,

Identikits
Page 34

see UK or Western women as people of low morals, prostitutes, sexual predators, temptresses of men. Equally, 'Western' women might be shocked by their first encounter with their Muslim counterpart wearing her hijab. Without dialogue, they may see the Muslim woman as subjugated, enslaved or even, perhaps, a religious fanatic or a potential suicide bomber. Clearly, with these attitudes, co-operation and trust are going to be out of the question.

These dress examples, that symbolise deeply-held beliefs, show how intensely emotional cultural tenets can be, and how much culture is a matter of the heart and not just of the head. This explains why cultural misapprehensions can sometimes lead to argument, violence and even, in extreme cases, the killing of individuals.

The quality of silence
Page 43

A valuable tool to help us reflect on cultural differences is provided by Richard Shweder [9]. He gives us four ways of perceiving, four standpoints:

- **Downward evolutionist** *I look down on this foreign culture/cultural practice.*
- **Upward evolutionist** *I look up to this culture/cultural practice.*
- **Universalist** *I see this culture/cultural practice as superficially different from mine but as being fundamentally the same.*
- **Relativist** *This cultural practice is different, but I feel fully comfortable about doing it myself in the context of the other culture.*

Four-way states of mind
Page 59

We can share this type of anthropological thinking with our students and help them to apply Shweder's framework to their own lives.

Culture within culture

Within national cultures there are sub-cultural practices (rules and behaviours that differ from the national patterns), which reveal a great deal about the community or group by whom they are used. The fact that they exist at all shows us how deep, diverse and how very complex even 'home' culture is. It is important to note that people living under the banner of any given nationality may have different ethnic backgrounds, different degrees of acculturation, as well as different amounts of respect for the culture within which they live. Because of this, they may have different ways of doing things, as well as recognising the national norm.

How annoying!
Page 70

Ways of behaving in the family and at school, as also in the workplace, are examples of sub-cultural practices. When we start a new job, we are aware that things may be 'done differently' by our new employers. Our children, when they come into contact with other families, tend to contrast what they see there with their own family experience.

The ideal student
Page 23

Gill:
I remember vividly being told, rather condescendingly, by an adolescent male that *his* mother had better things to do with her time than cook meals from *ingredients*! After all, supermarkets and ready meals were there to make life easier for women and, besides, his family always got to choose *what* and *when* they wanted to eat *individually*. The implication being that choosing to cook for my family meant I was wasting time, being old-fashioned and even perhaps a bit mean, not offering choice regarding menus or time of eating! Clearly, here a rather different set of values regarding food and mealtimes was in place in our two families. This boy had, as we often do, *judged* without thinking of the advantages of my approach to food and mealtimes, simply because he was used to something different.

We often fall into the trap of judging something negatively at first, when it is different from or challenges the way we know of doing things.

Classy meals
Page 44

It is worth noting again that even deciding what the word culture *means* is a matter of debate. In the past, culture was only talked about in terms of the arts and, then, only rarified forms, such as certain types of classical music or literature and the work of established 'safe' artists.

Gill:
One of my schoolteachers once urged us to go to a concert to watch a famous symphony orchestra play Beethoven's 9th because it would do us good to 'see a bit of culture'. Clearly this teacher only valued what we now know as 'high' culture – all our other cultural manifestations, which must have been apparent to him, didn't count for much in his estimation.

Cultural concepts
Page 54

Some art critics still make a distinction between these types of art and more modern forms, which are arguably more transient and appeal more (defenders of 'high culture' would say) to the 'lower classes', the 'masses', the 'popular audiences'. Good reviews in prestigious newspapers will help artists gain access to 'high-culture status', as will the patronage of a famous, respected art collector. People who view culture in this way would not consider other products of a society as belonging to the umbrella of culture. Sometimes these two standpoints are categorised as 'culture with a big C' or 'high culture' (the arts), and 'culture with a small c' or 'low culture' (other cultural products). Someone with this view may consider singers like Kylie Minogue and Madonna, iconic though they are, as belonging to the area of mass culture, pop culture: something altogether more dependent on fashion, much more ephemeral, and therefore of less 'cultural' value.

Questions of attitude
Page 79

When we look at the above paragraph we are aware that the words we are using may give offence. Language is inextricably tied up with culture, as we hope will become clear, and words are often culturally loaded, so if we choose one word rather than another, we give an initiated listener or reader a window into our own cultural heritage, or 'cultural capital'.

Cultural capital

Cultural capital, which leads to cultural power, is a sociological term, coined by Pierre Bourdieu and Jean-Claude Passeron (sociologists and philosophers)[10] in an attempt to explain under-achievement in French schools. Cultural capital includes knowledge, skill and education: in fact, any advantages a person has which can give them the expectation of a higher status in society. Parents provide children with cultural capital, for example, when they impart the attitudes and knowledge that help make the educational system a place in which their children will feel at ease and therefore can easily succeed.

Parental dos *and* don'ts
Page 36

Bourdieu subdivides cultural capital into three sections:

- **Embodied** *Embodied in the self, over time, through socialisation in the family and elsewhere. Ways of behaving and communicating effectively (or not) are learned in this way and become part of each individual character.*
- **Objectified** *Gained from things that can be owned: consumer goods, books, works of art ('high culture'), etc. However, Bourdieu would argue that cultural capital may only be gained from this ownership if we understand the articles 'in the right way'. Owning a painting neither makes us an expert on what the painter intended us to feel, nor indeed an expert on art in general.*
- **Institutionalised** *In the form of qualifications, certification from institutions.*

Teenage work
Page 36

We know that children, growing up in any country, will have very different expectations of their lives, depending on the kind of upbringing they have had, the attitudes of their parents, of their teachers and of the institutions in which they are educated. Bourdieu argues that the more cultural capital we have, the higher are our expectations, the more success we will have and thus the more power we can, as adults, wield in society.

The confusion of culture shock
Page 73

Thomas Sowell, a respected American economist [11], believes the cultural capital (attitudes and beliefs, in this case) that migrants bring to a new homeland is far more important in determining their fate than the homeland's economy, culture or politics. Migrants to a new country may feel some aspects of their own cultural capital are undervalued in the new environment and may actively seek to acquire new cultural capital that is more acceptable.

Learning the language, understanding the social rules (and the attitudes behind them), acquiring some of the products: all of these are obvious steps towards this aim. Often children of immigrants acquire cultural capital via school. Problems may then occur if the values learned in the school are not compatible with those of the parents.

Breaking rules
Page 30

> **Mario:**
> My Italian father migrated from Italy to the UK in the 1930s. In Italy, he had the cultural capital of a middle-class intellectual. His reason for migration was his marriage to an Englishwoman from a coal-mine-owning family. On arrival in the UK, he quickly began 'investing' in his wife's cultural capital, assimilating her language, her vocabulary, her attitudes, and her upper-class assumptions. In his English 'edition', my father was more upper-class and right-wing than he had been in the earlier half of his life, back in Italy. Sowell's and Bourdieu's concepts of cultural capital make clear sense to me when I think back to my dad.

Cultural codes

My values, your culture
Page 56

Shall I pour?
Page 35

As humans, we are always searching for meanings, and we will therefore *interpret* everything we see, hear, smell, taste, etc, in order to do this. Ferdinand de Saussure [12], the father of a field of study called semiotics, calls these methods of interpretation 'signs'. Signs can be sounds, texts, images, objects, odours, tastes or actions. These, it is argued, have no real meaning in themselves, but have meaning attributed to them by us. We experience the 'sign' and interpret it according to our own conventions of meaning, relating the sign to these, amassing a kind of database of our experience of the sign in our lives.

It is this idea of attributing meaning that is at the core of semiotics and the work of Ferdinand de Saussure, for whom a 'sign' is divided into two parts: the *signifier* (the form a sign takes) and the *signified* (the idea or concept it represents). This idea can be represented in the table below:

Signifier	**Signified**	
Car	Freedom Luxury	Financial liability Form of transport

Symbolic movements
Page 27

Gender words
Page 40

We may all receive signs in a slightly different way, as our reading of them will be influenced by our 'database', which we have amassed, growing up largely within a home culture, thereby establishing a 'code' (or language, incorporating our individual as well as national cultural beliefs and values) which we can use to interpret signs. It is inevitable, therefore, that what we perceive as reality is in fact culturally *encoded*, and thus becomes culturally *loaded*. Let us consider another example. For different groups of 'receivers' of the sign *Ernesto 'Che' Guevara*, there may be a wide range of differing responses:

Signifier	**Signified** (different for different receivers)		
Ernesto 'Che' Guevara	Freedom fighter Terrorist Army officer	Patriotic soldier Common criminal Bandit	Guerilla Cultural icon

Culture and language

As suggested above, language is inextricably linked with culture, but which comes first? Does the language we speak reflect our culture or is our world view determined, or at least affected, by the language we speak? The *Sapir-Whorf* hypothesis, named after two American linguists of the early twentieth century, would argue the latter: we make sense of our world by organising it into some sort of order. We do this by naming things, using language. Our view of the world, then, is going to be limited by, or at least shaped by, the language we use.

Softening what you say
Page 82

Sapir says (and we have highlighted the part that seems most significant):

'The fact of the matter is that the real world is to a large extent unconsciously built upon the language habits of the group. No two languages are ever sufficiently similar to be considered as representing the same social reality. The worlds in which different societies live are ***distinct worlds, not merely the same world with different labels attached****. We see and hear and otherwise experience very largely as we do because the language habits of our community predispose certain choices of interpretation.'* [13]

Don't let me be misunderstood
Page 75

Whorf adds:

'We cut nature up, organize it into concepts, and ascribe significances as we do largely because we are parties to an agreement to organize it in this way – an agreement that holds throughout our speech community and is codified in the patterns of our language.' [14]

Mario:
The word *kirei* in Japanese signifies both 'beautiful' and 'clean'. In English, beauty and cleanliness are two separate and distinct concepts and one does not entail the other. In Japanese, the concepts are intermeshed and 'kirei' is one of the keywords for understanding the Japanese way of thinking, at least if you come from an English-speaking culture. This seems to me to be an example of language enshrining culture and determining the way people are able to think, at least in so far as thought is verbal.

Snakes in the bushes
Page 41

Considered literally, there are two basic principles in the Sapir-Whorf theory:

- **Linguistic determinism** *Our thinking is determined by language.*
- **Linguistic relativism** *People who speak different languages see and make sense of the world differently.*

Taking the theory at face value, it would be difficult to translate thoughts, feelings and our understanding of our world into another language so that the speakers of that language see it in exactly the same way. Some theorists suggest that meaning will be changed as we repeat, or reformulate, statements to one another, even within our own language. If we paraphrase what someone says, then we may change the statement, colouring it with our own meaning. However, other theorists hold that we *can* always say what we want to in any language: that everything can be translated from one language into another. Karl Popper, the renowned philosopher, believed that there is 'essential truth' in every sentence which can be translated: 'even totally different languages are not untranslatable' [15].

Strange sounds
Page 78

While this may be possible in theory, as language teachers we do know that meaning is often lost in translation, sometimes with hilarious results, as in the classic examples taken from public notices translated into English.

Public notices
Page 76

From a Paris hotel	Leave your values at the front desk.
From a cleaner's in Bangkok	Drop your trousers here for best results.

Although today many theorists agree that, in its original form, the Sapir-Whorf hypothesis is a little extreme, there are important elements for us to note:

- Our outlook on life is influenced by the language we speak.
- The way we speak is influenced by our outlook on life.
- Our social context influences the way we use language.

In considering these three points, we are reminded of Michael Hoey's theory of *lexical priming* [16], where our initial experience of a lexical item 'primes' us for meaning in our subsequent encounters with the item.

The authors of *Culture in our Classrooms* believe that along with lexical priming (or perhaps as part of the process) we are also *culturally* primed. For example, if in our society we see 'black' not only as a colour but also a positive thing, we will imbue the word with only positive connotation.

The sound of silence
Page 43

Gill:
I was working with a group of African students on abstract nouns. I asked them to make an image of the word 'purity' using Cuisenaire rods. The group chose a single black rod, standing up on the table. Much later, when doing the same activity with a group of European students, I was surprised to find the group had chosen a single white rod. Clearly, then, black and white were seen and valued differently in these two cultures.

Culture and language teaching

In the teaching of modern languages, it has long been usual to include elements of culture and 'civilisation' as part of language courses in secondary schools, so, for example, a student in the UK studying French 'Advanced' level (for examination at the age of 18) would be expected to keep up with current events in France and know about French media, as well as education, legal, political, social and healthcare systems.

All this is praiseworthy, although it could be argued that what we learn about beliefs and behaviours from all this may be rather limited. More and more modern language materials are 'authentic', that is, taken verbatim from radio, TV and newspapers. This gives us more of an insight into national character via real language. However, again, this is limited. It depends what *kind* of authentic material, or how much of it, we expose our students to, as well how we decide to use it. (The latter is often limited by very tight curriculum restraints under which teachers have to operate.)

UK quiz
Page 86

Institutions and the internet
Page 86

Our point here is that learning lots of field-specific lexis and statistics won't help our students get into the mindset of the average French person. If anything, there is a danger of reinforcing stereotypes. There is a gap, if you like, between the information given about life/institutions and how things actually work at an anthropological, human level. For example, a secondary-level student of English in Germany or France may have learned about the class system in Britain and that the government has devised a method of defining class via our professions. At the top of the UK government-designed 'class tree' are owners of large companies, in Class 1, whereas the permanently unemployed are in Class 8 at the bottom (see the British Office for National Statistics website [17]). However, from these statistical frameworks, the student won't learn how social class is expressed through the clothes we wear, the car we drive, the language we use to describe everyday things, the newspapers or magazines we read, and so on. What is missing from this tightly curriculum-bound teaching of life and institutions is that it leaves aside the insights to be gained by a more anthropological approach.

The best day of the year
Page 32

Learning from the host family
Page 84

Cultural competence

In an attempt to address this issue, along with descriptors to assess *linguistic* competence, there is now a series of guidelines to help us assess *intercultural* competence (our ability to understand and function in other cultures), as part of the introduction to the Common European Framework of Reference for Languages [18]. However, these guidelines are subsumed within the framework of socio-linguistic competences.

A parallel project administered electronically by LOLIPOP (a 'Language On Line Portfolio Project' with an 'enhanced intercultural dimension', run by 12 partner universities across

Europe and seven target languages [19]) also endeavours to pinpoint competences, which are equally defined in 'can do' terms. A very abbreviated look at three examples taken from their six levels (A1, minimum – C2, maximum) gives an idea as to their range:

Success stories
Page 31

- **A1** (Basic user) I can show that I have some basic knowledge of the other culture …
- **B1** (Independent user) I can understand the reasons for the different values, beliefs and practices of the other culture …
- **C2** (Proficient user) I can interpret and evaluate people's behaviour based on many different cultural theories I have encountered …

UNESCO [20] has also compiled a different series of principles, covering similar areas, although they fall short of actually outlining descriptors.

Everyone, it seems, sees the need to somehow measure and assess our intercultural competence. The fact that there is a lack of hard descriptors shows us how complex this concept is. Language teaching has been getting nearer and nearer to the idea that linguistic competence involves students being able to function *appropriately* in their chosen foreign language. The problem for teachers is how to tackle the *appropriate* aspect *appropriately*!

Culture and the classroom

If we accept, then, that culture is a huge influence on the way we run our daily lives, whether or not we are aware of it, then there *are* things we can certainly do to help our students:

Codes of conduct
Page 64

- to become more aware of their target-culture norms and behaviours;
- to recognise and understand more about other cultural beliefs and norms;
- to look a little beyond cultural stereotypes and develop more empathy towards other cultures;
- in doing this, to develop a much more profound awareness of their home culture.

It is our hope that activities such as those in *Culture in our Classrooms* will move teachers towards achieving the above aims. Doing so will involve some of the different types of thinking listed below.

Reflecting

As teachers, we need to carry out activities to get students reflecting on and analysing culture(s). Such activities require students to stand back and examine what might seem to be small details – like movement – and, from this, extrapolate information regarding the target as well as the home culture.

The prince and the pauper
Page 80

The focus can usefully be on texts that contain incidents where cultural *misunderstanding* has occurred and where, via discussion of these, students will deepen their *understanding* of the myriad ways in which a situation can be read, depending on one's cultural standpoint. And on reflection, if honest with ourselves as teachers, we will probably find ourselves consciously, or more often unconsciously, 'adopting' all four of the positions outlined earlier that correspond to the theories of Richard Shweder.

Red card behaviour
Page 28

Sharing

Given that teaching in a monolingual, monocultural situation is becoming less and less common, it is also useful to encourage students to explore the cultural wealth of their own class group. If we want our students to think about and engage with ideas and beliefs that challenge them, that is, to teach them to listen without judgement, to share ideas without prejudice and start to empathise with people from different backgrounds who may have (and be happy with) a different set of beliefs, then we need to help them understand that one's home culture is simply a system of learned behaviour patterns and not the only way to do or see things. We do this by facilitating the sharing, and comparing, of information and experiences of home and other cultures.

One woman's story
Page 42

To sleep, perchance to dream
Page 37

Comparing

Comparison is crucial. When confronted with something new we tend to compare it with what we already know, from our own experience. We contrast different cultural products or norms with the ones we are used to in our home culture. If you like, we can only see and judge things from where we are in our own culture.

Who are you, teacher?
Page 22

So we can invite our students to speculate, to project. Members of a new class can even be asked to make lots of assumptions about their teacher's lifestyle. This sort of activity gets them to work as a group and, of course, they often like to gossip about their teachers!

On target!
Page 74

Preparing

Finally, we can't expect students to go blithely from their home culture to a target culture without a little preparation. And activities, of which there are several in Part B, which look at the behaviours and beliefs of an English-speaking country like the UK – in particular, but they are perfectly adaptable – can be extraordinarily helpful, allowing students to exchange information about each other's cultures as a prelude to (as well as during) visits.

Culture and content

On course!
Page 52

Language learning is an odd subject. You could say it is not a subject at all, in the sense that 'content' subjects like chemistry, history and physics are. Like music, language is a skill, a 'how'. The problem has always been to fill the *how* with a *what*:

- The powerful Content and Language Integrated Learning (CLIL) movement seeks to fill language teaching with the rest of the school curriculum.
- The humanistic movement seeks to use the students' own lives and interests as the 'what' of the learning (see *Teaching Unplugged*, by Meddings and Thornbury [21]).
- International coursebooks will often propose a 'what' of the sort you might find in a magazine or newspaper.

In *Culture in our Classrooms*, we are suggesting that a useful, engaging and emotionally relevant 'what' can be the differences and samenesses between cultures.

There are many more activities in Part B that we have not listed above: we invite you to investigate them, read 'what' they have to say – and see 'how' you can use them in your classrooms.

- Students are communicating something worthwhile as they look at the cultural features within their class group.
- They are communicating about something deep and compelling when they compare their own culture to that of the target or other languages.
- If their teacher is a foreigner, comparing that culture to theirs can be emotionally fascinating.

We propose this as 'content' because it is intellectually, emotionally and personally challenging for students, involving them at many levels and offering you, the teacher, the stuff with which you can 'hook' your learners.

We finish, then, as we began. Culture is everywhere. Where we are, where you are. Where you are from, where you are going. As you clamber onto our shoulders and, hopefully, enjoy the activities in *Culture in our Classrooms*, you will develop a wider and more positive personal perspective and you will see a much more generous horizon than we do.

References

[1] Kramsch, C 'The Cultural Component of Language Teaching' *Language, Culture and Curriculum* 8 (12) 1995
[2] Kramsch, C ibid.
[3] Hall, E T *Beyond Culture* Anchor Press/Doubleday 1976
[4] Brislin, R W (Ed) *Applied Cross-Cultural Psychology* Sage Publications 1990
[5] Kramsch, C op. cit.
[6] Hofstede, G *Cultures and Organizations* McGraw-Hill 2004
[7] Trompenaars, F *Riding the Waves of Culture* Nicholas Brealey Publishing 1997
[8] Fox, K *Watching the English* Hodder and Stoughton 2004
[9] Shweder, R *Thinking Through Cultures* Harvard University Press 1993
[10] Bourdieu, P and Passeron, J-C *Reproduction in Education, Society and Culture* Sage Publications 1990
[11] Sowell, T *Migrations and Cultures* Basic Books 1996
[12] de Saussure, F *Course in General Linguistics* Open Court Publishing 1983
[13] Sapir, E 'The Status of Linguistics as a Science' *Language* 5 1929. Quoted in *Selected Writings in Language, Culture, and Personality* University of California Press 1992
[14] Whorf, B L 'Science and Linguistics' *Technology Review* MIT Press 1940
[15] Popper, K 'Normal Science and its Dangers' In *Criticism and the Growth of Knowledge* Latkos, I and Musgrave, A Cambridge University Press 1970
[16] Hoey, M *Lexical Priming* Routledge 2005
[17] www.statistics.gov.uk
[18] www.coe.int/t/dg4/linguistic/CADRE_EN.asp
[19] www.lolipop-portfolio.eu
[20] http://portal.unesco.org/en/ev.php
[21] Meddings, L and Thornbury, S *Teaching Unplugged* Delta Publishing 2009

Reading

Kate Fox
Watching the English – The Hidden Rules of English Behaviour Hodder and Stoughton 2004
Passport to the Pub – The Tourist's Guide to Pub Etiquette Do-Not Press 1996
The Racing Tribe – Watching the Horsewatchers Metro Books 1999
We have learnt more about English society from Kate Fox than from any other single author. It would be marvellous if such in-depth anthropological books of general appeal were available about other cultures. Well-crafted and articulate.

Claire Kramsch
Language and Culture OUP 1998
Context and Culture in Language Teaching OUP 1993
Language Acquisition and Language Socialization – Ecological Perspectives Continuum 2002
A 'must' if you are serious about culture in language teaching. The writing is clear, convincing and a breath of fresh (cultural) air!

George Mikes
How to be a Brit Penguin 1984
Heartily funny: a classic.

David Hackett Fischer
Albion's Seed – Four British Folkways in America OUP 1989
The author deals with attitudes to money, women, sex, children, architecture, schooling and thirty more 'folkways' over the centuries. The most complete anthropological history we have yet read.

Craig Storti
Figuring Foreigners Out – A Practical Guide Intercultural Press 1999
The Art of Crossing Cultures Intercultural Press 1990
Cross-Cultural Dialogues Intercultural Press 1994
Storti's work is a rich source of short passages on culture and exercises that you can usefully use in your classroom. Ideal for work with upper-secondary students.

Robert Winder
Bloody Foreigners – The Story of Immigration to Britain Little, Brown 2004
The fascinating story of how London and then the rest of the UK absorbed the waves of immigrants that today make up a multi-ethnic society.

Steven Pinker
The Language Instinct – The New Science of Language and Mind HarperCollins 1994
An engaging and convincing argument, as well as a really good read!

Alvino Fantini
Exploring Intercultural Competence – A Construct Proposal Brattleboro (Vermont) 1995
Whether or not one agrees with this standpoint, it is interesting and thought-provoking.

Michael Byram
Teaching and Assessing Intercultural Communicative Competence Multilingual Matters 1997
Intercultural Competence (Ed) Council of Europe 2003
Instrumental in the construction of the CoE Framework of Reference for Languages, Byram sets out his stall meticulously. We learned a lot.

www.aber.ac.uk
The media pages are excellent, especially the work of Daniel Chandler: user-friendly, fascinating and instructive.

Round the world

Print magazines such as *English Teaching Professional* and online forums such as *Humanising Language Teaching* offer a window for sharing perspectives on both teaching and learning throughout the world.

And Delta, the publisher of *Culture in our Classrooms*, has a blog where you can post your comments and share ideas with us and with your fellow teachers: *www.deltapublishing.co.uk/development-blog.*

We have absolutely no doubt that both you and your students (so many different scenarios, such different cultures) will transform the activities we have written into something richer and better than what we propose. When you do, then let the world know!

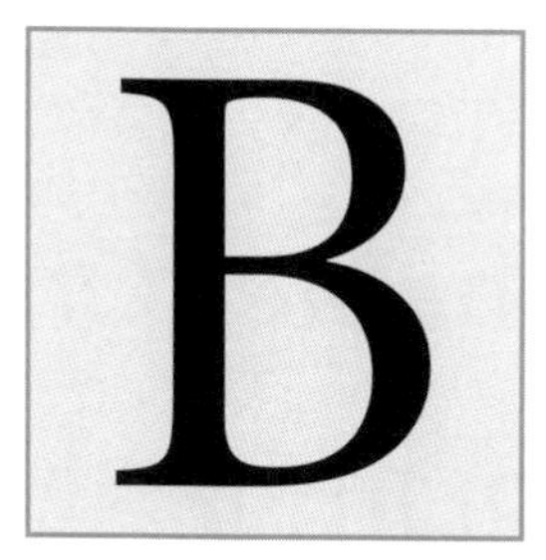

Culture in our Classrooms began by pointing out the all-present and all-pervading nature of culture. And the classroom is obviously no exception. Our pleasure in teaching is largely based in trying to understand our students not only on an individual personal basis but, equally importantly, as members of their cultural groups.

- Cultural matters are powerfully psychodramatic, they sit so fiercely, they are so emotional and so well-buried below the surface of consciousness. Cultural norms govern wide swathes of what we do and what we believe.
- The groups we belong to tend to regulate our unconscious and conscious existence: we 'introject' their values so firmly that we take them to be our own, individual values.

Culture in our language classrooms

Our students, and ourselves their teachers, belong to a classroom group, an environment which offers huge possibilities for raising awareness of these subterranean forces, as we address 'cultural content' while still accomplishing our roles as language teachers.

A more precise look at language, the cultural aspects of its words and discourse, provides further areas of communication, contact and even surprise.

Cultural issues can be the basis of whole courses – or the subject of individual lessons. And the frames that allow us to approach culture can range from the analysis of concepts and constructs, codes and conventions, diagrams and debates, surveys and statistics – to roleplays and simple (and not so simple!) reactions and responses to a single open-ended question.

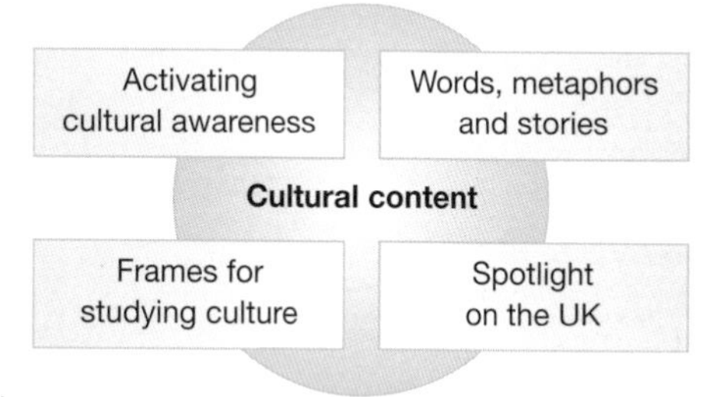

Even focusing on an English-speaking country like the UK, the subject of the cultural content of many a language curriculum or the target of many student exchanges, can be a touchstone for discussion and dialogue – creating more language and more awareness.

In other words, Chapter Four inextricably refers us back to Chapter One, across the threads of the intervening chapters. As readers, you are invited to view this book as a whole, taking and adapting from it what, where and how you see fit. As authors, we feel a little sad that our experimentation with the many ideas in Part B of *Culture in our Classrooms* is tapering to a close. However, we are buoyed up by the expectation that you will meet your students in new and exciting ways through these practical lesson scenarios.

Chapter One
Activating cultural awareness

A young Chinese person is walking with an older person and helps them across a busy road, taking their arm and steering them carefully and solicitously. The young Chinese does this automatically, just as any 'decent' person would in the Chinese quarter of humankind. The young person is unaware of doing something that is culturally governed – it is simply *normal* and, implicitly, universal.

Chapter One helps students to 'unpack' the very dangerous word 'normal' and to realise just how much the behaviour of people from other civilisations is culturally and unconsciously normed, governed and determined. Perhaps more importantly, the students come to realise how relative and how culturally determined *their own* behaviours and beliefs are. All of this they gradually discover through a variety of classroom activities.

Cultural categorisations

A warm-up to thinking about culture

Cultural content

Students start thinking about the cultural similarities and differences between their home country and other lands.

Procedure

1. Ask the students to work on their own and write down between five and seven ways in which their country is *different* from other countries (this can be other countries in general, or it can be *specific* other countries).
2. Now ask them to write down between five and seven ways in which their country is *similar* to other countries.
3. Finally, ask them to choose one region of their own country which is different from the national norm. They jot down five to seven ways in which it is different.
4. Group the students in sixes to explain their three lists to each other.
5. Bring the students back together and ask them to tell the class the single most interesting thing they have learnt during this session, letting their discoveries lead to a general discussion.

Postscript

Our colleague Sheelagh Deller used part of this technique to get a *Culture of the UK* course going and was pleased with the participants' response. She inspired this activity.

My story

Who I am and where I come from

Cultural content

Students exchange information about their cultural backgrounds and realise that another person's cultural focus may be quite different from theirs.

Preparation

Have ready a model 'cultural autobiography'. It could be your own, or you could use the example below. Give out the text and check understanding.

Lesson One

For homework, ask the students to write notes, or a paragraph or two, about themselves, following the model. Encourage them to provide as much detail as possible.

Lesson Two

1. In the next class, pair the students so that you get the widest possible cultural variation, but ensure they are happy to work together. Get them to exchange their texts and read them.
2. Ask them to write down as many questions as they can to clarify their partner's text, and return the texts plus the questions to their partner.
3. The students tell their stories to their partner, incorporating the answers to their partner's questions.
4. When everyone is ready, elicit one or two stories.
5. Focus on the questions that were asked for clarification – often we take for granted information about our culture and thus forget to bear it in mind!

I was born in the North West of England. My father was a northern working-class, protestant patriarch, and my mother a Londoner and a middle-class, Jewish matriarch. I was exposed to two radically different cultures and different languages.

My mother's family were Russian-Jewish refugees. When I stayed with them I didn't always understand the languages they spoke, but I loved the food they cooked and the beautiful songs they sang. The warmth and closeness of this part of my family will always be with me.

We lived on a council (subsidised, state-owned) estate in Blackburn, Lancashire, which was very white and working class, but I went to school with lots of Indian and Pakistani children and was great friends with them. I often visited them in their homes and was exposed to more differences – language, food, clothes, religious practices and probably much more, besides, that I'm not even aware of!

Who are you, teacher?

Let's find out a bit about you, shall we?

Cultural content

Students are allowed to speculate about you, their teacher, and learn something about your cultural background.

Preparation

Think of some areas (like the ones below) that you are happy to reveal about yourself. This is a good activity for when you have been with your group for no more than a day or two, and if you are of a different nationality from your class.

Procedure

1. Tell the students they are going to speculate about *you*!
2. Divide them into groups of three or four and give them some headings to help them make some notes. For example:
    - my hobbies
    - the newspapers I read
    - what I earn
    - my daily routine
    - the car I drive
    - my family life
    - my house
    - the food I like
    - the drink I like
    - my free time
    - my attitude to money
    - my attitude to politics
    - my attitude to education
    - how I'd be (I am) as a parent

    (Obviously, only give them headings for areas you'll be comfortable to talk about.)
3. Give them 10-15 minutes to write notes for themselves and then discuss their ideas within their groups. Try to get them to agree, as far as possible.
    - **A monolingual group** This will be easier, as your students will often have the same preconceptions about you, viewed from their cultural standpoint.
    - **A multilingual/multicultural group** There may be big differences.
4. The groups share their ideas with the whole class. At this point, they have to decide on what they think the truth is – about you. If protocol permits, leave the class, wait outside and give them 10-15 minutes to talk. If not, be as unobtrusive as possible. You can use this time to write some notes of your own, under the same headings.
5. When everyone is ready, the students call you back into the class and tell you what they think. You let them know how right/wrong they are. Ensure that you link what is true about *you* to general truths about *your culture*. For example:
    - *Actually, teachers are not very well paid in my country.*
    - *Most people of my age would be buying/renting/sharing a house/flat.*
    - *Outside big cities, very few people use public transport.*

    This part of the lesson could be a short phase or a detailed, deep discussion.
6. For homework, get the students to write a note to you, telling you what they learned about you and what (maybe) particularly surprised them.

Postscript

This activity is adapted from an idea given by Katie Plumb in St Petersburg.

The ideal student

A teacher's view

Cultural content

Teachers in different cultures want students to behave and to believe in different ways.

Preparation

Copy the Iranian text opposite, one per student.

Procedure

1. Give out the Iranian reading to the students (perhaps in a first lesson) and ask them to underline each opinion that they feel would correspond to the idealised view of a student that a teacher might hold in their own culture.
2. Run a plenary session in which people round the class read out those Iranian sentiments that a teacher from their cultures would also cherish.
3. Ask them to pick out the statements their teachers would *not* agree with.
4. Now tell the students they have 20 minutes to work on their own and write two profiles of the 'ideal student':
   - No 1 is the profile seen by an old, conservative teacher from their culture.
   - No 2 is the view of a young, modern teacher also from their culture.
5. **A monocultural class** Group the students in fours to read each other's texts.

   A multicultural class Group the students with people who share their culture, and ask them to read each other's texts. Then re-group them so they read the texts written by people of a different culture.
6. Run a plenary session in which people forget about teacher idealisations of the student role and speak, instead, about how *they themselves* imagine 'the ideal student'.

Postscript

The text was adapted from a text written by Abdollah Baradaran and Mehdi Khademzadeh and taken from *General English through Reading*, Zaban-e-Daneshjoo Publishing House, Tehran, Iran.

An ideal student

Students must realise their duties. They are the future administrators, soldiers, statesmen, and teachers. They should try and become ideal students so that they can play their roles in a good manner.

An ideal student is one who has true discipline. He knows the value of self-control and does not like useless and foolish activities. He applies his sense of judgement and does not follow others blindly. He follows the right way of life and refuses to follow the wrong path.

He is obedient and respectful. He respects his parents and teachers. He cannot even think of any disrespect to his elders. He doesn't boast of his learning, scholarship or achievement in any other field. He is devoted to his duty. He does not believe in wasting the first months of the year and then working overtime in the last months. He works regularly and continuously.

He is always interested in increasing his knowledge. In his free time he is in the library reading papers, magazines or other useful periodicals. He has an interest in the affairs of the world and keeps in touch with them.

An ideal student has love for his religion and country. He is not without the noble sentiments of patriotism. He realises that he has to contribute to the growth and progress of his country.

If the country is confronted with some dangers, he steps forward to render the best help possible. He does not allow any anti-national element to harm his country.

What embarrasses you?

From methodology to match-making

Cultural content

Students explore the 'loss of face' rules in a classroom in their culture and compare these with those in other cultures.

Preparation

Make copies of the 'teacher behaviours' list opposite for each pair of students.

Procedure

1. Pair the students, give each pair a list and tell them to go through the behaviours and rank them (from 1 to 5) in embarrassment caused to students:
   - 5 is *'very embarrassing'.*
   - 1 is *'not embarrassing at all'.*

   Ask them to think of what people in *their culture* would typically feel, rather than what they feel themselves as individuals.
2. Round off with a plenary discussion of the three or four teacher interventions which are generally agreed to be the most embarrassing.

Postscript

In most cultures, some of the discussion of loss of face will hinge on the gender of the teacher and of the student. Let this come out in the paired conversations and incorporate it into the final class discussion.

The list is adapted from a set of statements written by Faranak Abbaszad Tehrani, of Ankara. He was writing in the context of Iranian and Turkish university students.

• Your teacher asks you a question when you are not ready.	
• Your teacher never asks you any questions. Do they know you exist?	
• Your teacher reads out test scores to the class and yours is low.	
• Your teacher keeps on correcting your pronunciation mistakes in a discussion lesson.	
• Your teacher tells you to translate a ten-page article for next week.	
• Your teacher interrupts you when you are asking a question, and brings up something new.	
• Your teacher offers to drive you home.	
• Your teacher mentions that they have seen you at a concert with your boyfriend/girlfriend.	
• Your teacher accuses you of not fasting during a period when one is meant to fast.	
• Your teacher points out that you will not pass the end-of-semester exam and that you will fail.	
• Your teacher congratulates you on your clothes.	
• You know you have given a good presentation, but your teacher says it is no good.	
• Your teacher promises to find you a good husband or wife soon.	

The world as I see it

Of course we're the centre of the universe!

Cultural content

We see the world, even geographically, from our own perspective.

Preparation

If you are working with a single-nationality group, you will ideally have photocopied maps from different student nationalities so that your students can see and compare these with their own. You might consult ancient atlases (perhaps Chinese or Japanese) or 'distorted' modern tourist brochures.

Have some sheets of unlined paper ready for the students to use.

Procedure

1. Hand out sheets of unlined paper, one per student.
2. Ask everyone to draw a map of the world. Reassure the students that you aren't looking for artistic masterpieces or perfect accuracy.
3. When everyone is ready, put the maps on the wall and get the students to look at them all and comment on what they see. With a single-nationality group, put your photocopied maps up, too, so that your students can see and compare these with their own.
4. Hold a feedback session focusing on the significance of our perception of ourselves as the 'centres' of our world, and how this shapes our 'world view'.

Postscript

What usually happens is that each student will have put their own country in the centre of the map and will be very surprised that other students have done the same – and 'got it wrong'!

A student of Gill's from North Africa

Gill's son, just back from Australia

Beliefs behind behaviours

The why behind the what

Cultural content

Students identify the cultural beliefs that lie behind the ways they behave.

Preparation

Make copies of the 'Four behaviours' text for the students (or write them on the board). As you read through this activity yourself, note the 'Key' section.

Procedure

1. Tell the students the following:

   When you meet a culture that is new to you, what you mostly see are the things people do. You see how they walk, hear how they talk, notice whether they are punctual for meetings. When you get in a taxi, you feel how they drive, etc. These are all behaviours, and yet underlying nearly all behaviours in a culture there are beliefs and states of mind. There will be a 'why' behind the 'what'.

2. Give them two examples of UK behaviours:
   - In a shop, people put money in the other person's hand, while in some other cultures money is placed on a surface between the two people.
   - Street beggars generally have a hat or tin for donations. People put their offering in the container. In Italy people tend to give beggars money in their hand.

3. Tell the students to stand up and work in pairs, first practising giving money into the hand and then onto a surface.
   - In pairs, one partner sits on the floor, roleplaying a beggar.
   - They try the Italian and the British way of giving money.
   - They should notice how they feel in either case.

4. Ask the class:
   - How did they feel in both cases?
   - What is the belief behind the British way of putting money into the hand, and what do they think about it?
   - How does it compare to their own behaviours/ beliefs in this situation?

5. Group the students in fours or fives, and ask them to have a look at the four behaviours outlined opposite and compare them to parallel behaviours in their own culture. What differences are there between them and, in both cases, what are the beliefs behind the behaviours?

Four behaviours

1. Host: *Would you like some more meat?*
   Guest: *Not really … no thank you.*
   The host removes the food.
2. Some British houses have front gardens, between the road and the front of the house. It is very rare to ever see anyone sitting, reading or talking in this space.
3. The bus comes. The British mostly stay in an orderly line and board the bus one after the other without jostling or pushing forward.
4. In crowded situations, like travelling on underground trains in the rush hour or in a crowded lift, it is unusual to see people making eye contact with each other.

Key

Example situation:
In a British shop, putting the money in the assistant's hand demonstrates a mutual affirmation of trust and honesty. The British state of mind behind putting money in the beggar's container is one of embarrassment about giving and being seen giving, because 'Maybe I shouldn't be giving money to this person'.

Situation 1:
In the UK, respect for the other requires us to take someone at their word. If they say they aren't hungry, the British will believe them!

Situation 2:
British people tend to use their front gardens as a 'buffer zone' between the outside world and their world.

Situation 3:
What lies behind this is a sense of fairness: first come, first served.

Situation 4:
Even in crowded situations, by avoiding eye contact, the British allow each other the feeling of more personal space. It's a way of offering their travelling companions more respect.

Images in different cultures

I see things my way

Cultural content

A stereotypical roleplay opens students' eyes to the way different cultures imagine really simple things differently.

Procedure

1. Number the students from one to four.
   - The **Ones** are to mentally roleplay being a person living in the Arctic Circle.
   - The **Twos** are to mentally roleplay being a person living next to the Atlantic ocean.
   - The **Threes** are to mentally roleplay being a person living next to a huge African river.
   - The **Fours** are to mentally roleplay being a person living in the Gobi desert.
2. Now dictate this sentence:
   The woman came down to the shore – she saw a fisherman.
3. Tell each student, *in role*, to draw a picture of the scene the above sentence makes them think of.
4. Tell all the Ones, the Inuits, to come together and compare their drawings, while all the other numbers do the same – the Twos together, the Threes together, the Fours together.
5. Now tell the students to re-group in fours, with one person of each number in each group. They show and explain their pictures.
6. Draw the class together for an exchange of reactions and a plenary discussion.

Postscript

The teacher can optionally personalise these roleplays, using place names the students will know.

We learnt this cultural perception activity from Helen Wood, D'Overbroeck College, Oxford, UK.

Symbolic movements

A gesture is worth 1,000 words

Cultural content

Movement and gesture can make students aware of different aspects of culture.

Preparation

Get ready by reflecting on the following:

- a basic posture/gesture to represent a family member
- a basic movement to represent your local area
- a basic movement to represent your country

Procedure

1. Clear space as you would in a drama class – tables and chairs to the walls, if possible.
2. With the students in a big standing circle, make *your* first gesture and tell the class this symbolises a person in your family. Everybody imitates your gesture as you do it a second time. Now explain what this gesture means to you.
3. Get several students to produce a gesture that represents a member of *their* family, for everybody to imitate. Get them to explain what each gesture means.
4. Now allow the students to form small, culturally homogeneous groups and to each decide on gestures to represent their region and their country. In each place, they need to explain the meaning of the gesture. Ask each group to now decide on a common-to-the-group gesture to represent their country.
5. The groups come back into the big circle and, one by one, they show the others their group gesture to represent their country and explain what they mean by it.
6. Ask the students to form a circle of chairs and allow time for comments on the representation of the country/ies.

Postscript

Expressing meaning through movement will sometimes bring up from the unconscious both thinking and feeling that the person was not previously aware of.

Red card behaviour

I didn't mean to offend you

Cultural content

How easy it is to be upset by someone else's 'natural' behaviour, their proxemics and their use of gesture and voice.

Preparation

Prepare ten small red cards for every student and one 'cultural offence' card each. On each offence card, you put one of the sentences in the box below.

Procedure

1. Give ten red cards to each student and one *cultural offence* card – and tell them not show this to anybody.
2. Tell the students what they will have to do:
   - They are going to get up, move around the room, find a partner and have a conversation about a past holiday.
   - If a partner 'offends' a student, according to their offence card, the student gives them a red card, but without any explanation.
   - Once *two* red cards have been given in a pair, or after two minutes have passed, the conversation stops, and they both go off to find a new partner.
   - Everyone should speak to about six people.
3. Get the students to write up their 'cultural offences' sentences on the board.
4. Allow a reactive discussion to ensue. Ask the students if they can imagine which cultures the 'dislikes' might belong to.

Postscript

The 'red card' in this activity takes knowledge of football behaviours for granted – an interesting cultural detail in itself! We learnt this activity from Nicki Kukar: it is one of a large family of awareness-raising cultural roleplays developed in the USA over the past 40 years.

- I hate being physically touched in a conversation.
- I hate people who talk to me but stand an arm's length away, so I keep trying to move nearer to my partner.
- I hate people who stand right up close to me, so I keep trying to move back, away from them.
- I hate people who use a lot of gesture as they talk.
- I hate people who never move their hands when they talk.
- I hate people who look into my eyes as they talk.
- I hate people who don't look into my eyes as they talk.

Groups I belong to

Is this racism?

Cultural content

Fostering awareness of inclusion and exclusion.

Preparation

Think of three groups you belong to. Prepare to describe what is positive for you in this 'belonging' and how people *in* the group feel about people *outside* the group.

Procedure

1. Tell the students about three groups *you* belong to. Explain the positive features of these belongings and describe how members of your groups feel about non-members.
2. Ask the students to work individually and think of three groups *they* belong to:
   - Ask them to write a list of three benefits in belonging.
   - Ask them to list three feelings they have towards people outside each group.
3. Group the students in fours to compare their thoughts.
4. Finally, open a discussion in plenary or, alternatively, you might like to set this essay title as homework:
   'Racism is horrendous because it is natural.'

Racist, me?

I heard somebody say ...

Cultural content

Does what people say reveal what they really think?

Preparation

Have one copy of the sentences opposite per five students.

Procedure

1. Give the class, in groups of five, the true statements opposite, explaining that they are given by some British 15/16-year-old schoolchildren about racism.
2. Ask them to choose three or four statements that someone they know well might easily say and to prepare arguments that *this person* might use to back up these statements.
3. Get them to discuss their statements – using the arguments they have prepared. Remind the students that they are not necessarily presenting their own views!
4. When it seems appropriate, get the whole class back together and ask the students for feedback on how it felt to argue a different point of view – and whether they felt any sympathy with the argument they had defended.

Postscript

Often students are quite shocked to find that although they don't consider themselves to be racist in any way, they do, in fact, hold views which may seem racist to other people! It may be that, despite our best efforts, we are all racist to some extent.

- I think racists are ignorant.
- I think racists just don't understand other cultures.
- I think it's just that some people don't want to share their country with other people.
- I think unemployment and competition for jobs makes everything worse.
- The asylum seekers at my school have language support workers who sit with them in class. It must cost a fortune. Why can't they learn English somewhere else, first?
- I don't think the school is racist, but some kids are.
- It's not a question of racism. We can't afford to let anyone else into our country.
- It must be awful to have people being horrible to you because of the colour of your skin.
- I get really angry when lessons get held up because the asylum seekers can't understand the teacher.
- When kids from other countries who come to our school get bullied because they aren't British, I think 'What does it say about us?'. I mean, what must they think of us all?
- I've seen a boy at our school get bullied because he's an Arab. They called him 'Bin Laden's boy' and were hitting him. I watched and did nothing. I was scared.
- I hate the way asylum seekers use vouchers at the supermarket. It's like the government doesn't trust them to use real money. If the government sends out that message, it's easy to see why the public sees these people as second-class citizens.
- I get really cross when I see these people getting money from the government and working 'on the side'. There are poor people who were born here who should get help before we start with anyone else.
- The problem is that we don't learn about other cultures at school. Take History – it's mostly British and European; same with Geography. Religious Education is a bit better, but still mostly Christian. We don't get the chance to have any multicultural awareness.
- I get angry when people talk about racists. What do they mean, anyway? If being scared that your jobs, your houses, your state benefits will be taken away and given to people who just come here for that, then all my family are racists. OK, we need to share stuff out, but it's our country – we need to put money into getting it working properly first.

Me and my culture

Do I always agree with everything?

Cultural content

Students come to notice where they are out of step with their own culture.

Preparation

Think of a community *you* belong to (for example: the school/the town/the region/your country) and prepare to tell the students about some of your beliefs that are different to the majority views – the consensus beliefs. We have included two examples below, to get you thinking.

Procedure

1. Tell the students to what extent you fit in with the beliefs of the group you have chosen to speak about, and to what extent you are out of step with some of those beliefs. Give clear examples.
2. Ask them, working individually, to think of two or three disagreements they have with societal beliefs (school/church/workplace/country) and to jot down some notes about each one. Allow ten minutes for this. (During this thinking/writing phase, you may need to help individual students clarify their thoughts and come up with vocabulary, etc.)
3. Group the students in fours to share their 'differences'.
4. At the end of the group discussions, ask representatives of each group to write their most important points on the board. You might want to use this format:
   - My society thinks …
   - But I believe that …
5. Use these points to hold a general discussion with the whole class.

Mario says: *In my country it is more usual for women to do the cooking, cleaning and washing, but in my home it is me who does it.*

Gill says: *In my country it is still traditional for men to be the main 'breadwinners'. However, in my family I'm the main breadwinner.*

Breaking rules

Who made them anyway?

Cultural content

Identifying cultural rules by looking at the ways they are transgressed.

Procedure

1. Tell the students that you are going to dictate – in a whispered tone – some rule transgressions from the Oriya culture in Southern India. See below.
2. Now whisper-dictate the sentences.
3. Group the students in threes to identify the rules that have been broken and to decide how they feel about them.
4. Allow them to share their ideas/feelings in plenary, if they wish. Are there any similarities or parallels between Oriya and home cultures?
5. Give the students marker pens and ask them to fill the board with rules from their culture(s) that are often transgressed.
6. Allow time for a whole-class discussion in reference to the writings on the board. (In a multicultural class, some of the rules will need explaining.)

Postscript

These Oriya rules are from 'The Big Three of Morality (Autonomy, Community, Divinity)', by Nancy Much, Manomohan Mahapatra and Lawrence Park, in Richard Shweder's *Why Do Men Barbecue?*, Harvard University Press, 2003.

1. A woman cooked rice and wanted to eat it with her husband and his elder brother.
2. A young married woman went alone to see a movie without telling her husband.
3. A letter arrived addressed to a 14-year-old son. Before the boy returned home, his father opened the letter and read it.
4. One person in the family eats beef regularly.

Transgressions

1. She thought she could sit down with the men.
2. She failed to ask permission.
3. He was violating the boy's privacy.
4. Eating beef is wrong.

Success stories

Wow! I got it right

Cultural content

We need to realise how good we can be in the area of cultural adjustment.

Preparation

Read Mario's cultural success story below, but prepare to tell *one of your own*. Your students will relate to *your* tale of cultural learning or appropriateness because they know *you*. It is better to avoid using a third-party text.

Procedure

1. Tell your own culture success story and explain that you will be asking the students to tell some of theirs. Explain that culture success stories can be about acting well in the context of another *family*. It can also be dealing with people from another *region* of one's own country.
2. Invite one or two of the more extrovert students to tell the class a story of their own, then group the class in fours to tell the stories that came to their minds.
3. Round off with whole-class feedback on the satisfactions of getting some aspect of another culture right.

Postscript

As an alternative, you can model a cultural *failure* story yourself, and then ask the students to tell theirs.

> I was in a car in Istanbul, sitting next to my host, a Turkish publisher.
>
> We had stopped to pick up a female colleague of his. I hopped out of car and went to sit in the back seat.
>
> Ahmet turned round and said: *'Mario, I wonder why you have changed seats.'*
>
> *'Well, so Bahar can sit in the front seat.'*
>
> Ahmet then said:
>
> *'She may be a bit embarrassed when she comes down. I mean, she sees you as our guest and you are older than she is. In Turkey, people respect age.'*
>
> Once Ahmet's words had sunk in, I realised what I had to do and slipped back into the front passenger seat. Just in time. Enter Bahar.
>
> Thank you, Ahmet, for your brilliance as a discreet and gentle teacher of culture.

Things I like

Three cheers!

Cultural content

Students become aware of and express aspects of a foreign culture that they feel good about.

Preparation

Prepare to tell the students about three aspects of a culture you know well and that you really appreciate.

Procedure

1. Dictate the appreciation below by a psychiatrist from India, married to an Irish woman, who had spent ten years in England.
2. Now tell the students that when asked who he would cheer for in an England versus India cricket match, the Indian man tried to get round the question but then said: *'Of course, India!'*
3. Pose the question:

   Given the information you have, where do you feel this man belongs?
4. Now tell the students some positive aspects of a culture you know.
5. Ask them to think of a culture they have experienced by listening to songs, by reading, by watching TV or by living with the people of that culture, and to think of three or four positive aspects of it. It could also be a local sub-culture, like a different racial group, a sports community (eg skate-boarders), etc.
6. Tell the students to write half a page of notes mentioning the positive aspects and then group them in fours to share their ideas.

Postscript

You can do the same activity, but about *negative* aspects of the other culture. This is usually much easier, but may be less useful.

The text is taken from *The Independent* newspaper, 08/01/04.

> *I feel British when I am restrained in my emotions. I am no longer emotionally expressive or loud as I was when I was in India. I have become far more diplomatic in the way in which I express my emotions. In India, as a doctor, I was supposed to know everything. I had to be a god. Here in the UK it is acceptable to say 'I don't know'. I can be human.*

The best day of the year

A happy time

Cultural content

Students explore and share information about cultural festivals.

Preparation

Be ready to describe your favourite day in your cultural calendar. It would be helpful to have some pictures, music, perhaps special food, etc, to help you illustrate the importance of this day. It could be a national festival or a rite of passage celebration. Remember to include:

- the history of the event
- why it is particularly important to you
- how it is traditionally celebrated
- how you celebrate it (if this is different)
- the underlying beliefs that people are celebrating

Have ready some sheets of A4 paper.

Lesson 1

Tell the students about your special day and ask them to prepare a similar talk, but without reference to the beliefs or values behind it, to be presented to the class. If a number of students want to do the same festival, let them work together. The preparation of the talk can be done for homework or during class time. If your students have access to the internet, they can use this to aid their research.

Lesson 2

1. Give the students five minutes each – to give their presentations, show pictures, costumes, food, etc. While they listen, ask the others to note down the fundamental values they think underpin each festival.
2. On the sheets of A4 paper, write one festival name on each sheet. Hand out some sticky notes (one per festival) to each student. Ask them to write the values behind each festival and one comment they wish to make.
3. When they are ready, ask them to post their sticky notes on the relevant sheets.
4. Hand these sheets back to the relevant presenters and ask them to comment on the accuracy of the underlying beliefs. If appropriate, they could also comment on the comments.

Postscript

With a large class of individual presentations, you could ask every fourth student – but making sure that these are not all the 'best' ones.

Alternatively, spread the presentations over more than one class, so that all the students can see their preparation work suitably rewarded.

Two women and a funeral

Mourning time

Cultural content

Students explore the expression of emotion in the face of death.

Procedure

1. Tell the class you will read them a short paragraph about a funeral scene. Explain that it deals with two women who mourn in different ways. One shows *desperation and anger*, while the other is *stony in her tearless silence.* Put these two phrases on the board.
2. Tell the students their task will be to note down as many keywords and phrases as they can but to do this immediately *after* you have finished reading.
3. Read the paragraph below slowly, rhythmically and clearly. The students then write the keywords they have retained.
4. Pair the students and tell them to reconstruct the text word for word, using their pooled keywords.
   If this is the first time they have done a 'dictogloss' activity they will be struggling. Offer them a second reading – get their attention and read again, fairly slowly.
5. After most of the students have reconstructed as much as they can, invite one person out to the board, *without* their text. The other students then tell them what to write. You stay right out of the writing-up process.
6. Give the text to a student to read out slowly, so the 'secretary' at the board can put any mistakes right.
7. Ask each student to write about how feelings are expressed in their community when someone dies. Tell them this page of writing will be private. (Observe students discreetly but carefully, as these can be moving moments.)
8. Round off the lesson by asking how the students think different cultures do their typical mourning processes.

I remember two women at a funeral: there was one, who came from the Italian South, and she was tearing her clothes, wailing and keening, giving full vent to her desperation and anger. There was another, half German, half English, silent, stony, erect, all in black in her tearless silence. Two women – worlds apart.

Buffer zones

Home sweet home

Cultural content

How different cultures view the relationship between home/private space and the outside world.

Preparation

Download a number of images of dwellings from around the world and print them out. You might include images like those in the list below to think about.

Write a short text for each image you have downloaded. An example might be:

> *This home has a large front garden, between itself and the road. There is also a large door and curtains. All of this maintains the privacy of the occupants.*

Copy your texts and cut them into strips. Put the pictures up on the board or lay them on tables. Put all the strips of paper on a table, so the students can read them. If you are teaching a large class, you might want to make multiple copies and have your students work in smaller groups.

Procedure

1. Get the class to look at the pictures and decide which items of information match the pictures. They should then place the 'information strips' by the appropriate pictures.
2. When everyone is ready, you can reveal the correct answers.
3. Ask your students to consider their own homes. How is the 'buffer zone' created between their home and the outside world? Ask them to write notes or draw pictures to represent these buffer zones.
4. Get the students to share their information in groups first, then get each group to report back to the whole class for a general discussion.

- French homes with shutters
- American homes with curtains and front yards
- UK houses
- European flats/villas
- African/Indian rural dwellings
- Houses on stilts above water

Notice details such as:

- Are the dwellings open/closed to the outside world?
- Can people easily see into the buildings or not?
- How is the privacy achieved?

Looking through windows

Does where I live define who I am?

Cultural content

Students speculate on what housing reveals about societies, exploring the cultural value systems that rule our speculative comments.

Preparation

Have ready a variety of pictures of different kinds of housing. You may get these from estate agents or the internet, or have photographs of your own. The images may be from housing in the target culture or from several cultures. What's important is that you know, for example:

- the standard of living of the inhabitants
- how many people would normally share it

If you prefer, you could have prepared handouts, providing information on each of the images you have chosen.

Procedure

1. Divide the class into groups of four or five and ask each group to choose a picture.
2. Each group should decide together:
   - how many people live in the building
   - who they are
   - what jobs they might have
   - what they earn
   - what they think
   - what their routines might be
   - what their attitudes are to their children, jobs, religion
3. When everyone is ready, get each group to present their ideas to the whole class, dealing with questions from the other students as they arise.
4. Share the information you have prepared (either orally or via your prepared handouts) and see if the students can match the information to the correct images.
5. Have a final discussion focusing on what led the students to come to the conclusions they did and how this caused them to speculate on or judge (accurately or inaccurately) the behaviour and status of the inhabitants. For example, a person looking at a South African township house may think only one or two people live there and may be shocked to find that a family of six or seven or more live in it.

Identikits

You are what you wear

Cultural content

An exploration of symbolic dress codes.

Preparation

Photocopy the passage in the first box opposite.

Procedure

1. Ask the students to read the passage you have prepared and then dictate the questions to them.
2. Group the students in fives to give their answers to the questions.
3. Finish with a general discussion about the symbolism of the way people present themselves.

In many countries the military, nurses, policemen, workers in fast-food restaurants, musicians and judges wear uniforms. People have always shown their identity by things they wear, right through history. A few examples:

- Canon law in the Greek Orthodox Church requires that priests should wear beards.
- In the English Civil War, the King's men wore their hair long while the Parliamentarians cropped theirs – the Cavaliers and the Roundheads.
- In the 1970s, in the UK, a case was brought against a Sikh for not wearing a motor-cycle helmet. He was unable to because of his uncut hair bound up in a turban.
- In 2004, the French Lower House voted by 494 to 36 to ban all ostensible religious signs and forms of dress from state primary and secondary schools. This meant that Christians could no longer wear visible crosses and Muslim girls were no longer allowed to cover their hair with the traditional headscarf.
- Some pubs in London ban men wearing ties from coming in and ordering drinks.

- In your country, who wears uniforms? What do people feel about each uniform? What are the associations with each uniform?
- What do people wear to symbolise their status (for example: the rich, the religious, teenagers, etc)?
- How many different groups have you belonged to and do you belong to? Have you, or do you, wear anything to show your belonging?
- What do we think of as 'naked' and what do we think of as 'dressed' (for example: some women feel naked if they haven't got their make-up on and some feel naked if they aren't wearing their chador)?
- What are the cultural rules for hair? For females? For males?
- Is wearing perfume acceptable or desirable for both genders? Do some perfumes have more status than others?
- How important do you feel these matters are a) for you personally b) within your culture?
- Write two questions of your own about the symbolism of what is worn.

Take comfort!

Just like mama used to make

Cultural content

An exploration of the context and diversity of 'comfort food and drink'.

Preparation

Be ready to talk about your own 'comfort foods', foods that give you a sense of OK-ness, ease and familiarity. Choose some current comfort foods/drinks and some from when you were younger.

Procedure

1. Tell the class about your former and current comfort foods and drinks. Explain why you specially like these foods, their associations for you, etc.
2. Ask two or three students to tell the class about theirs. Choose students from different cultures or, if the class is 'monocultural', choose people, if possible, from different regions/suburbs/areas.
3. Ask each student to make a list of *former* comfort foods or drinks and *current* comfort foods/drinks. Ask them to underline any items that they consider many people in their culture would also find reassuring and comforting.
4. Organise small groups of four to six students so they can compare their lists. Group them as culturally heterogeneously as possible.

Postscript

This can be a powerful activity with people who are currently away from their own home cuisine. Think of the yearning for well-cooked rice among Japanese living among 'other-country people' (*gai-koku-jin*) and that desperate desire for potatoes of a British person living in a rice-eating culture. The stomach can be central in homesickness. How many Brasilians abroad would kill for a black-bean and pork *feijoada*, or a German person for some compact rye bread?

Shall I pour?

Drinking rites ... and wrongs

Cultural content

How simple actions can have many different cultural meanings.

Preparation

Take a jug of water and a glass to class.

Procedure

1. Pour the water from the jug into the glass. Pour it back. Do this two or three times in silence. These actions set the scene for what happens later in the activity.
2. Dictate the sentences below to the class and ask each student to write three sentences about the drinking rules in their own family.
3. Now ask them to write three sentences about the drinking rules in other situations in their society.
4. Group the students, as far as possible, in culturally heterogeneous groups of four to six people, and ask them to read what they have written.
5. The groups write three of the most interesting rules from their group up on the board.
6. Let this lead to a general discussion.

- Two Japanese men are drinking *sake*. The first man fills the second man's drinking bowl. The second man then takes the bottle and fills the first man's bowl.
- We are in a 'gentlemen's club' in London. Dinner is over. The decanter of port wine passes round the table and each man fills his own glass.
- A Danish dinner party. When someone wants to drink their wine, they propose a toast and they all drink their wine together.
- When a toast is proposed in Russia, everybody drinks the vodka in their glass to the last drop.
- In a UK pub, one person offers drinks to the group they are with. At an appropriate moment, another person will get up and pay for the next round.

Teenage work

A new computer? Get yourself a job!

Cultural content

Students get to think about and discuss central concepts, such as independence, money and work.

Procedure

1. Dictate an appropriate questionnaire, following the model below but modifying the questions according to your students. For example:
   - ***Did** you work as a teenager? **Did** you want to?*
   - ***Do** you work as a teenager, or **would** you like to?*
2. Group the students in threes to answer the questions. Group them as culturally heterogeneously as possible.
3. Regroup them into sixes to share and discuss their answers. When they are ready, ask each group to tell the class some of the things they learned from their discussions and which they found:
   - interesting
   - surprising
   - shocking
   - amusing
4. Open up into a discussion about the attitudes different cultures have towards paid work.

- Did you work as a teenager? Did you want to?
- Nearly nine out of ten students in the US take part-time work, as salespersons, babysitters or in fast-food chains. How do you feel about this?
- What are the advantages of early work?
- What are the disadvantages?
- As a parent, do you think it's a good idea for your children to work while at school? Why/why not?
- Are there differences between work in the family and work outside?
- Does work bring the teenager independence? If so, from what?
- What qualities does work foster in the teenager?
- Can work alienate a teenager?
- Please write two questions of your own.
- To what degree do you find this questionnaire appropriate to your culture?

Parental *dos* and *don'ts*

How things change!

Cultural content

An exploration of how parental injunctions change from culture to culture and generation to generation.

Preparation

Prepare some of the *dos* and *don'ts* that you heard as a child. To get you thinking, below are some of ours.

Before the lesson begins, write some of your childhood injunctions on the board.

Procedure

1. Ask the students to read what's on the board and explain that these were things you heard as a child.
2. Invite them to fill the board with injunctions *they* heard as children. You may need to help with translation problems. (If this is a multicultural class, ask the students to write their nationalities next to their injunction, to see if a cultural pattern emerges.)
3. Ask the students to read what's on the board and iron out any language difficulties.
4. Allow the class to react to what is on the board, in plenary.
5. **A monocultural class** Ask the students to work in pairs and make a list of things they say, or might find necessary to say, to *their* children.

   A multicultural class Ask the students to work with a partner from their own or similar culture to do the same.
6. While the students are doing this, clean the board. When they are ready, ask them to fill the board with their injunctions to their children.
7. Finally, ask them to imagine what they think would be on *your* list! Ideally, you should leave them to do this alone.

- *Look at me when I'm talking to you!*
- *Don't slouch. Put your shoulders back!*
- *Distraction will be your ruin!*
- *Speak when you're spoken to!*
- *Don't drag your feet: shoe leather costs money!*
- *Keep your elbows off the table!*
- *Don't talk with your mouth full!*
- *Don't eat with your mouth open!*

To sleep, perchance to dream

How good is sleeping alone?

Cultural content

Students explore the beliefs in different cultures, including their own, of the 'OK-ness' of co-sleeping within the family.

Preparation

Copy the questionnaire opposite for each student.

Procedure

1. Tell the class whether you slept on your own all through your childhood, and also tell them what you decided to do in this area with your own children. If you have none, then describe what another member of your family has done with their children.
2. Have the students sit together in groups of four to six. If you have students from different cultures, make sure the small groups are culturally heterogeneous. Ask each group to elect a questionmistress/master (QM).
3. Take the QMs out of the room and give them the questionnaire. Tell them that, when they return to their groups, they should read the first question and let each person answer orally. They should follow this procedure for all of the remaining questions. They should keep mental tally of the answers, as there will be a reporting phase.
4. The QMs return to their groups and administer the questionnaire.
5. Bring the whole class together and ask the QMs to report on the most striking things they heard in their group, before rounding off with a general discussion.

Postscript

This activity is based on 'Who sleeps with whom revisited', by Balle-Jensen and Goldstein, in Richard Shweder's *Why Do Men Barbecue?*, Harvard University Press, 2003.

- Was sleeping with your parents normal for children in your family, or did each child have a separate room?
- Did you sleep away from your parents but with your brothers and sisters, cousins, etc?
- How old were you when you first slept alone?
- In the USA, 25% of African-American children sleep with one or both parents between ages 0 and 5 years old. What do you think the percentage would be in different groups in your country?
- In Appalachian Kentucky, USA, among working-class folk, 71% of children between the ages of 2 months and 2 years sleep with their parents. Would you have liked to sleep with your parents at that age?
- Approximately 50% of urban Japanese children of 11 to 15, back in the 1960s, slept in the bed of their mother, their father or of both parents. If you had early-teenage children, how would you feel about them co-sleeping with you?
- In Japan, sleeping arrangements emphasise interdependency and the Japanese feel that sleeping with others reduces the tension between male and female and between the generations. How do you feel as a member of your culture about these Japanese beliefs?
- One Appalachian mother said that mother and child should sleep together: *'How can you expect to hold onto your children in later life if you begin their lives by pushing them away?'* What would your mother have felt about her view?
- What do you see as the major disadvantages and risks of parents and children sleeping together?
- Each of you, please:
  - Write a question about co-sleeping that you want other members of our group to answer:

    ....

    ....
  - Ask us your questions.

Rules for life

Do you always do what your mother said?

Cultural content

Students become aware of how they learned some of their own culture, how much of it they still accept and what part of it they would pass on to the next generation.

Preparation

Have ready a list of 'rules' you were given as a child. For example:

You must give up your seat on the bus for an older person.

Procedure

1. Ask the students to write a list of all the 'good behaviour rules' they were given by their parents/family/carers when they were children.
2. Ask them to categorise the rules under the headings:
   - Not important
   - Important
   - Very important
3. Put the students into small groups so that they can exchange the information. Allow a few minutes for this.
4. Now ask them to highlight 'rules which have changed' as they have got older and to tell their groups what the changes are.
5. Ask them to tell their groups which rules they would keep (or have kept) for their own children.
6. If appropriate, open this discussion out to the whole class, focusing on the changes to the rules and what has brought these about.

Postscript

The idea of questioning a culture's age-old 'good conduct' rules is, in itself, a culture-loaded idea. Inevitably, Gill and Mario write from the matrix of their Western, individualistic culture.

The title of this activity is deliberately ambiguous. It could mean 'rules for living your life' or 'rules that are for life – that are difficult to shake off'.

All change!

Listing what's becoming obsolete

Cultural content

Students notice the ways in which the world is changing and the diverse ways their own communities are changing.

Preparation

Be ready to give three or four examples of 'things that are becoming obsolete' in *your* community. To get you thinking, below are some things we have noticed are changing.

Procedure

1. Write up this heading on the board:
   Things that are becoming obsolete
2. List three or four things that you have noticed are fading into the past.
3. Tell the students to write lists of changes that they have noticed taking place in their societies. They work on their own and write at least 15 things.
4. Now ask them to fill the board with their thoughts and ask them to underline the ones they think are international.
5. Working in pairs, they put the items on the board into categories. Tell them that each category must be given a heading. (They are free to choose the categories they want.)
6. Ask some of the pairs to describe how they have categorised the items, as well as their rationale in each case – and discuss.

Postscript

We learned this activity from Christine Frank. For more list-writing ideas, see *Creative Writing* by Christine Frank et al, Helbling Languages, 2007.

- Public payphones are less and less used.
- In the UK, front gardens are being replaced by carports.
- Hitch-hiking is happening less and less.
- Newspapers are being replaced by websites.
- Paying for things in cash is less common.
- Phrases like 'Jolly good' and 'Gosh' are nearly dead.

Chapter Two
Words, metaphors and stories

We know that you, our readers, most likely have a strong linguistic intelligence and are therefore probably fascinated by the language of words, metaphors and stories. Did you know that a 'fox hole' is the area under a desk where telephone calls can take place without interruption? Or that an 'ant hill family' is a family arrangement where children move back in with their parents and they all work together towards their mutual financial goals? (More on *The Guardian* newspaper website: www.guardian.co.uk/books/booksblog/2009/dec/15/best-words-of-the-decade.) Both these items are expressions that entered English in the 'noughties' of this century.

This chapter caters for language, and love of language, but from the viewpoint of culture. Remember, though, that not all your students will be initially as enthusiastic about words and language as you are!

A lesson I learned

Now I understand!

Cultural content

By exchanging and analysing stories, we generate awareness of how we can find good in another culture.

Preparation

Be ready to tell your students a story about a lesson that you learned from another culture and that was important to you. To get you thinking, there is a story of Gill's below. However, a story of *yours* will have much more impact on your students than one from someone they don't know.

Procedure

1. Tell the students your story and check comprehension.
2. Ask them to think of a *positive* lesson they learned, about their own or another culture, that has stayed with them. You might need to monitor/help with vocabulary, etc.
3. When the students are ready, put them into small groups so that they are as culturally-mixed as possible. Get them to tell each other their stories. Questions may be asked for clarification, so that everyone is clear what both the stories and the lessons are.
4. Depending on your class size, ask some of the groups to tell one of their stories to the class. The storyteller should be someone different from the original teller.
5. Allow time for discussion in plenary of whatever opinions these retellings provoke.

When I first went to work in the Middle East, I didn't understand why men and women couldn't be together at social events, so I didn't go to parties. After a while, I went to one – with my female students. I was amazed by the fun-loving, intimate and very relaxed atmosphere and I had a very good time. I also realised that, back in the UK, I often chose to do things with my women friends anyway.

The lesson I learned was that, although it's important for me to choose how I spend my time, actually I often choose what Middle Eastern custom requires. For some time afterwards, every time I arranged to see female friends I would hear my Middle Eastern students' voices in my ear, saying *'See? See?'*.

Gender words

Which expressions feel more male or female?

Cultural content

How loaded (both culturally and personally) gender-related words can be.

Preparation

Choose 15 words or expressions:

- Five that you feel are typical of femininity in your culture
- Five that are typical of masculinity
- Five that are applicable to both sexes

For example, take the word 'strong'. For you, is this a femininity keyword, a masculinity keyword or generic? To start you thinking, there is a short list below.

Procedure

1. Ask the students to rearrange the seating so that females are one side of the class and males on the other.
2. Call out the words, mixing the ones you think are female, male or both.
   - If the women/girls think the word you call out especially applies to females in their culture, they stand up.
   - If the men/boys think the word called out is male-associated, *they* stand up.

   Have a secretary at the board who writes down the words called out and the number of people who felt it was female and the number who felt it was male.
3. Draw the students' attention to how they voted and let this lead into a class discussion.

Variation

Ask the women to stand when the words you call out seem *male* to them and the men to stand up for *female* words.

Postscript

We learnt the gender aspect of this activity from a sociology lecturer at Liverpool Community College, UK.

compassionate	macho	warm
home maker	bossy	friendly
fashion conscious	superior	happy
gossip	player	poor
strident	dominant	political

Snakes in the bushes

Animals as metaphors

Cultural content

Students explore the metaphorical role of the snake and the mouse across different cultures.

Preparation

Be ready to give the class some examples of 'snake' metaphors and proverbs from different cultures. There is a list below with some of them.

Also have any snake metaphors you know from your own culture ready to share.

Procedure

1. Write up on the board some snake metaphors and sayings from various cultures.
2. Put the students into groups of four to six, with as much cultural diversity as possible in each group, and ask them to think of any snake metaphors or proverbs *they* know.
3. Wipe your examples off the board, and ask the students to fill the board with their examples: in their own languages and in English translation.
   - What is the explanation of the meanings of their sayings?
   - What characteristics do they think snakes possess to have attracted such metaphors?
4. Now ask them to brainstorm the qualities of a *mouse*. What kind of sayings/metaphors are associated with this little animal in their mother tongue? (In English we say: 'poor as a church mouse', 'quiet as a mouse', 'Are you a man or a mouse?', etc.)

Postscript

We learnt about *yabu hebi*, or 'bush snake', from *The Japanese Have a Word for It*, Boye Lafayette de Mente, Passport Books, 1997.

- In English, a *snake in the grass* refers to a person you can't trust, whose appearance is deceptive.
- In the Old Testament, it is written that *the serpent is the craftiest of the creatures of the field*. 'Craftiest' here means 'cleverest'.
- *'And the brazen serpent that Moses put atop a pole that the Jews in the wilderness only needed to look at, to be cured of snake bite.'* (Old Testament)
- In Japanese, there is a proverb, *yabu hebi ni marimasu yo*, which means 'that will turn into a snake in the bush' or 'you're just stirring up trouble'.
- In Western culture, the Ancient Greeks used the snake as the symbol of medical science.

No bushes, no snakes

Roleplay role-reversal

Cultural content

There are always two sides to a story and sometimes both are 'right'.

Procedure

1. Dictate the text below.
2. Explain to the students that they are to imagine it is the next day and that they are the college President. The President has just heard of the uprooting of the bushes and writes a letter to the group of Indonesian graduates.
3. Explain that each student is to roleplay the President and write a three-paragraph letter to the graduates. Give ten minutes for this.
   - When they have finished the President's letter, they hand it to the person on their *right*, and so on round the class.
4. Every student now has a letter from the college President. Tell them that they are all now to roleplay the spokesperson of the Indonesian group.
   - They have ten minutes to write a three-paragraph reply to the college President.
   - When they have finished, they hand it to the person on their *left* (in other words, back to the person who wrote the President's letter).
5. The students now resume their role as college President and write a 'reply to the reply'.
   - When they have finished, they exchange papers with the person on their right so they can read the whole correspondence again.
6. Round off the lesson with two or three groups of three reading their letters to the whole class.
7. Ask the students how they felt as they role-reversed from one cultural stance into the other.

Postscript

This 'snake story' was reported by Craig Storti.

In Indonesia, people avoid growing bushes round dwellings, as they don't want to make it easier for snakes to come hunting for food in their houses. A group of Indonesian graduates arrived on a college campus in New Hampshire, USA, where they were to live for six months. Their dormitory was surrounded by thick, leafy bushes. They tore the bushes up and piled them a good distance from the dorm.

One woman's story

How I got here

Cultural content

Students face the realities of immigrant/refugees, who are offered the space to tell their own stories – if they want to.

Preparation

Photocopy the text below for your students.

Procedure

1. Tell the students that they are going to read the story of a woman's autobiographical journey. Give them the text.
2. Allow the students to read the story and discuss it in pairs/small groups. The discussion must *only* concern the text, *not* students' own experiences, at this point. Give them the questions opposite to help focus their discussions.
3. Take feedback on the questions in plenary then ask:
   - Do you know anyone who may have had a similar experience?
   - Have you a story you would like to share?
4. If appropriate and if students wish, let them tell their stories to the class. In a home-culture group, a discussion on attitudes to immigrants could usefully take place.

Postscript

When we heard this story, it was very moving and upsetting to imagine a real person we all knew having to go through this kind of experience. So be aware that you and your students might be upset and shocked to find that members of your class have experienced similar things. However, following an activity like this, greater understanding and closeness is likely to break out all over the group!

- What do you think this woman looks like?
- Can you say anything about her character?
- Could you imagine this woman as a relative or friend?
- How do you feel about what this woman experienced?
- How do you feel she was treated by her new country?

My journey

My journey is a journey through time and emotions, as well as real travel.

When I was a child, I lived in a happy world. I loved and trusted my family and neighbours. I grew up in a community of people from different ethnic backgrounds but we respected and liked each other. My village was a safe place. I married and had children and never thought I would move away.

When the war started I learned to fear for the first time. I lived with different shades of it every day. My neighbours were wary of me and I of them. Suddenly we were enemies and people I had loved all my life were calling me filthy names. Along with my fear there was hurt and anger, too.

Then when the war came to my village I learned to hate … My husband was tortured … This was agony for me to see and yet I found myself feeling grateful that they didn't kill him! I knew we had to escape.

We left our village and started walking, pushing my husband along in a wheelbarrow. That was a time of real despair. I didn't know what would happen to us. I just knew I had to be strong for my husband and my children.

I don't want to talk about how we came to England, but I felt great hope and expectation on our way here. The soldiers had told us we would be looked after and said we were very lucky. I felt lucky. My husband would get medical treatment and I would be able to study … and my children would have an English education! I imagined English people would be kind and that London would be a wonderful place with big parks and elegant people. It was a very exciting time.

When we arrived it was cold and raining. We were treated roughly. First we were placed in a hostel with many refugees … some were our enemies. We were terrified, but I never let it show. Sometimes people would call us names. I had vouchers to buy food so everyone knew at the supermarket that I was an asylum seeker, even if my English was better than the cashiers'!

I didn't have any money and there were no elegant parks or people where we lived! I went to school with my children to help them with their English and I asked again and again for a home for my family.

When we were given our flat I was so happy I thought my heart would burst. When I saw it, I was really depressed. It was in a huge tower block with lifts that smelled of urine. I was afraid for my children, but we moved in. For the first time, we had a safe place to live and we could relax. The relief was enormous. I learned to hold my head up and walk past the drug dealers and bad boys on the estate where I lived. I was always afraid, but I didn't let anyone see. I enrolled at my local college and learned to be a teacher of English. I worked hard and I succeeded. My husband gradually got better and was able to do a little work, so we had some real money. We are learning to be hopeful again and to think about the future …

The quality of silence

Still waters run deep

Cultural content

An exploration of some meanings of silence.

Preparation

Prepare to read or tell the story below – telling is much more effective. Prepare copies for the students if you so wish.

Procedure

1. Tell the students the 'kite story' and elicit the following:
   - the value the kite placed on the silence or noise made by the mothers
   - what both mothers were doing, apart from being silent or noisy (staring, fussing around)

   It is important to establish that there is usually something else going on that shows the quality or meaning of the silence – body language is often key.
2. Ask the students whether the kite's interpretation of the mothers' reactions is something they recognise from their own cultures. If not, how would they change the story?
3. Ask them to explain how the meaning of the silence is expressed in the story, as far as they're concerned.
4. Ask them (in groups of three or four) to brainstorm situations where silence is 'used' in their own cultures.

The Kite
An Igbo tale from Nigeria

Once upon a time, the kite sent her son to hunt for food. He looked down and saw a duck with her brood. The young kite swooped down and carried off one of the ducklings in his beak.

The mother duck stared at him but said nothing.

The kite flew back to his own mother and she asked him how the mother duck had reacted. He replied that she had merely stared at him and said nothing.

The mother kite said: *'You take this duckling right back to his nest. His mother's silence may mean she is planning something.'*

The young kite obeyed his mother.

Then, on his flight back, he saw a hen with her brood. He swooped down again and carried off one of her chicks. The mother hen clucked and spluttered – she fretted, cursed and fussed around.

When the kite got back to his mother she asked him what the hen's reaction had been.

'Oh mother, she made a terrible fuss.'

'Ah, then there is nothing more she can do', and the two kites tore the chick to pieces.

The sound of silence

How does it make you feel?

Cultural content

Students analyse their cultures' attitudes to silence.

Procedure

1. Ask the students to shut their eyes, stay silent for two minutes and simply quietly open their eyes when they think the two minutes are up. Then ask different people round the class how they had felt during the silence. Accept all their answers with equal, non-judgemental interest.
2. Group the students in fours to tell each other about silences they remember: calm ones, frightened ones, embarrassing ones – whatever.
3. Tell them you are going to dictate to them the way that Southern Apache Indians in the US tend to be seen by non-Apache Americans:

passive	*uncooperative*
sullen	*anti-social*
unresponsive	*lazy*
withdrawn	*hostile*
stupid	
4. Ask the students how a person who says very little is judged in *their* culture. Is silence seen as positive or negative?
5. Tell them that in Finland, silence is generally much appreciated. Put the Finnish proverbs or phrases below up on the board.
6. Allow time for the students to react as a whole class. Ask them if they have sayings in their own cultures about the nature of silence and talkativeness.
7. Thinking of the two views of silence above, ask the class where their cultures come on the silent–talkative continuum and discuss in plenary.

Postscript

This lesson is based on ideas in *Perspectives on Silence*, Deborah Tannen and Muriel Saville-Troike (Eds), Ablex, 1985.

Listen a lot, speak a little.

One word is enough to make a lot of trouble.

One mouth, two ears.

A fool speaks a lot, a wise man thinks instead.

Brevity makes a good psalm.

One word is as good as nine.

Classy meals

Quite a mouthful!

Cultural content

An encounter with a set of 'class indicator' words – the complex set of words designating meals in UK English.

Preparation

Copy one 'quizmaster's sheet' per student.

Procedure

1. Divide the class into groups of five or six. And ask each group to send up a quizmaster (or mistress) to your desk. Give each of them a copy of the quizmaster's sheet.
2. Now ask each group to send you a 'secretary'. Tell these people it is their job to take notes of the correct answers the quizmaster reads out.
3. After the groups have worked through the quiz, ask the class the questions again yourself. Get responses from the 'secretaries'.
4. Ask the students to work in small groups and compare 'meal words' in English to equivalent words in their own language. Give them a chance to express their reaction to the class complexity of this set of words. Share your own feelings about this area of English vocabulary.
5. Give everyone a copy of the quiz.

Quizmaster Ask your group the questions below. Allow one minute for your classmates to come up with their answers. Time the minute. Ask your classmates to write their ideas down but do *not* comment. At the end of the minute, ask them to read back what they have written.

Then read them the correct answer slowly – read it twice, so the secretaries can take notes. Move on the next question.

---

1 How many words are there in British English for the full evening meal?

Answer

- The working-class word is TEA.
- The middle-class word to describe the working-class evening meal is HIGH TEA.
- The lower-middle and middle-class word for a full meal at 7.00 pm is DINNER.
- The upper-middle-class and aristocratic word for an informal evening meal is SUPPER. These people say DINNER for a formal evening meal.

2 Are the words *English breakfast* and *continental breakfast* class markers?

Answer

No, they are class neutral, though today the British tend to have large breakfasts only at weekends and on holiday. Most Bed and Breakfasts offer 'FULL ENGLISH BREAKFASTS'.

3 What are the two class-marker words used for the midday meal?

Answer

The working class say DINNER while the middle and upper classes talk about LUNCH.

4 What do teachers and students in state schools call the midday meal? What about in expensive private schools?

Answer

- In state schools the children either eat SCHOOL DINNERS or PACKED LUNCHES.
- In the private sector (9% of UK children go private) they eat LUNCH.

5 Who uses the words *afternoon tea* for a light meal at 4.00 pm? Who uses the word *tea* for the same meal?

Answer

- The working class call a cup of tea with sandwiches and cakes eaten at 4.00 pm AFTERNOON TEA.
- All the other classes call this TEA.

6 Where does *brunch* fit into UK 'class speak'?

Answer

It doesn't. The word BRUNCH for a late-breakfast-cum-early-lunch is an idea imported from Australia/USA.

Middle-class assumptions

Life's good!

Cultural content

Students gain insight into the mindset of a middle-class Danish couple and, using this as a comparison, comment on middle-class assumptions in their own countries.

Preparation

Copy the Christmas email snippets, one per student. Also copy the Chairperson instructions for each chairperson you will be appointing.

Procedure

1. Group the students in sixes; do so as culturally heterogeneously as possible.
2. Appoint a Chairperson in each group and give this person the sheet of email snippets of the Christmas email. They also need their instructions.
3. The Chairperson is to explain the situation and ask the initial questions. They then proceed to read the first snippet to their group, read them the questions and then encourage each of the other five members of their group to react to what has been read. The Chairperson then moves on to the next snippet.
4. When the groups have worked through the email, give each student a copy of the text and ask them to re-read it.
5. Round off the session with a general discussion.

Chairperson: This is a round-robin email sent by a retired school teacher to his and his wife's friends. The message tells these people about the year that is just finishing. The couple are in their late sixties.

- Would a retired teacher in your society write this kind of email to their friends?
- If so, what would be the content of the email?
- Would people in your culture object to this kind of letter?
- If so, why?

Snippet 1

The only problem that J and I have is that we cannot complain about anything except that we haven't got time enough for all our activities. We are still surprised about how we found time to do a proper job before we retired. Every day is full of new and exciting challenges and activities.

- Can you think of people in their late sixties whom you know in your society with attitudes like those of this couple?
- If not, what would typical attitudes be like in this age group?

Snippet 2

Having our houses in S, in L and on the North Sea coast means that there is always something to look after and to mend … . We even spent three months in L this summer and because of my wife's hard work in the garden she got it under control.

- How near the top of your social pile would you need to be to own three residences?
- Would you find these same keywords in the thinking of similar people in your society?
  to look after *to mend* *hard work* *control*

Snippet 3

As you may remember, J had an artificial ankle in 2005 and we are very happy that the operation was a great success. But we are also very surprised that implanting an artificial ankle is not more used here. Most hospitals just make the ankle stiff by nailing and screwing the bones.

- How would people in your culture feel about the 'can-do' attitude of this couple?
- What sort of complaints would an 'old' couple where you live make about medical care?

Snippet 4

D and J, our granddaughters, are without doubt the climax of this year's delights and wonderful experiences. It's a fantastic feeling to recognise the development of the two girls and J and I enjoy playing hide and seek, singing songs or just reading stories to them. The meaning of life is much clearer to us than ever.

- Do grandparents in your culture feel, think and speak like this?
- What similarities and differences do you sense?

Note the difference

Variety is the spice of English

Cultural content

Students access the cultures of various Englishes via detailed awareness of people's oral expression.

Preparation

Organise for a native speaker of English to come your class for a 20-minute period (Canadian, Singaporian, Nigerian, Irish, UK, US, etc). Ask the person to come prepared to talk about two possible topics they are passionate about.

Procedure

1. Introduce the speaker and ask them to outline very briefly the two topics they have to offer. Ask the class to decide on the one they want to hear about. Do this by a show of hands.
2. Now tell the students to take notes of anything the speaker says that *they* think they would not say when *they* speak English. They can be very simple things like '*um, huh, you know, sort of*', etc. They should have a page of notes at the end of a 15-minute talk.
3. Invite the speaker to start and during the talk *you* note down things that the speaker says which *you* would not say, for reasons of age, gender, language variety differences and, of course, 'idiolect', etc. Make a second list of things you feel your students should focus on.
4. When the talk is over, group the students in fours to comment on the talk and to share the notes they have taken. (Some speakers like to stay during this process and are amazed to hear how they themselves speak!)
5. Share your own first list with the students. (If you are a native speaker, students are often surprised that you speak differently from the speaker. Here you can usefully introduce the concept of 'idiolect'.)
6. Point out the things they may have missed in their notes, things from your second list. Also ask the students to discuss what they have learnt about this speaker's culture.

Postscript

Students find this kind of note-taking hard, so we suggest you invite different speakers in to lead this activity at regular intervals. You can find natives speakers on DVD, native-speaking colleagues, language assistants, foreigners who have come to your city and, across Europe, Erasmus students.

If you bring a dozen different speakers to your class over a period, your students end up with notes on a dozen different native idiolects, amassing a unique 'corpus' of language that they effortlessly link to the people they have met, so that the utterances they have noted down are shot through with the cultural and personal specificity of each speaker.

Grandpa's story

The past is another country

Cultural content

An introduction to the difference in stories from culture to culture and also from generation to generation.

Preparation

Prepare to start the class by telling either a story about a grandparent of yours or a story that your grandparents told you about themselves.

Copy the Bangladeshi story below for the students.

Procedure

1. Tell your 'grandpa story' to the class. Then give the students the Bangladeshi story to read, and help with any difficult words.
2. Ask them to write a three-paragraph 'grandparent-focused' story of their own.
3. Group the students in sixes to listen to the stories. This is interesting in a monocultural class, but can be even more fascinating in a multicultural situation.

Postscript

The text is taken from *I'm a Teacher, Get Me Out of Here!* by Francis Gilbert, Short Books, 2004.

I remember Grandpa picking snakes out of a bucket. He smelt of wet, muddy fields and always carried around a long gnarled stick, which he called his wand. He would poke and investigate the snakes with the stick, talking to them, soothing them and laughing with them.

I would go with him to market to sell the snakes. The women always said he sold the freshest snakes in Sylhet. They would ask him to kill them before their very own eyes so they could be sure the snake was fresh. Then they would take them home and make snake curry with them.

Snake makes good, fishy-tasting curry. I would recommend it. But you don't have it here in England: you will have to go to Bangladesh for that.

Woolly words

Lexical legacies

Cultural content

Students explore a word set that derives from one period of UK history, leading to an exploration of similar sets of words in their mother tongues.

Lesson One

1. For homework, ask the students to each google these phrases:
   - cloth-eared
   - mutton dressed as lamb
   - homespun wisdom
   - a wolf in sheep's clothing
   - the black sheep of the family
2. Ask them to come to the next class with three examples of sentences in which the phrase/word is used. (For example, they will discover that *cloth-eared* collocates to the right with negative nouns like *git*, *twerp* and *idiot*.)

Lesson Two

1. Ask the students to fill the board with the internet sentences they found contextualising the five expressions you gave them, and then dictate the story opposite.
2. Pair the students and ask them to underline all the phrases they can find connected to wool, spinning and weaving. Check comprehension of the metaphorical meanings.
3. Explain that these 'wool words' date back to the UK wool trade in the 12th to 15th centuries. Ask the students to work together in small groups of the same mother tongue, to find word sets in their own languages that relate to a historical period, to the climate of their land, to the economics of their country, etc. For example:
   - Arabic has many camel metaphors and proverbs.
   - Spanish has sets of words of Arabic origin in fields like architecture, engineering and administration.
4. Each mother-tongue group reports back on a set of words/phrases/proverbs they have identified and 'teaches' the class a couple of examples, translated into English.

Postscript

This activity is designed with a typical early 21st century European secondary class in mind, with perhaps 30-50 percent immigrant students in it. At one point, the 'immigrants' are invited to teach the 'natives' about their cultures of origin.

We came across our set of words in *Bloody Foreigners – The Story of Immigration to Britain* by Robert Winder, Little, Brown, 2004. There are others we have not incorporated into this activity: *sheepish*, *fabricating evidence*, *a plot unravelling*, *shepherd's pie*, *weaving falsehoods*, and so on.

> And then there was my grandfather, a dyed-in-the-wool conservative. He wasn't rich either – but when he was young he'd had the wool pulled over his eyes and they fleeced him – took him for his last penny. Never talked, though, about the crooked things *he'd* got up to.
>
> The yarns he used to spin about those distant days of his youth – he'd go on and on and I have to admit I sometimes lost the thread of what he was saying. Granddad was clear as a bell about the old days, but his notions about things round him tended to be a bit woolly.
>
> He passed away last month – broke his leg in three places and died of the complications. The bones simply would not knit. I miss him and his homespun wisdom.

New words for new times

Fashion is not just for clothes

Cultural content

Students are encouraged to look at new features of UK life by meeting the new words that evoke them.

Preparation

Make copies of the list of definitions for each student.

Procedure

1. Ask a student with good hand-writing to write up the words or expressions below, all over the board.
   - grief tourist
   - touch in / touch out
   - hand-me-ups
   - al desko
   - cyber slacking
   - to miswant
   - infomania
   - earworm
   - marmalade dropper
   - me time
2. Ask the class to say or speculate what each one means.
3. Give the students the definitions list and group them in fours to decide between them the following:
   - Which of the social phenomena described by the words were around when their parents were young?
   - Which of these social phenomena exist in their country, as well as in the UK?
   - What are the neologisms in their mother tongues that express these phenomena?
4. Round off the activity with a plenary discussion.
5. As homework, you can ask the students to investigate more socially interesting neologisms by visiting the following website: www.macmillandictionary.com.

Postscript

The source for the words studied in this activity is *Macmillan Words of the Year* by Kerry Maxwell, 2006. The definitions opposite – at that time new words – were googled on 16th December, 2006.

It is interesting to compare the results for November 2009, below. Most of the words have many more Google references, with **al desko** going from 2,100 to a staggering 340,000. Of course, we have to take into account that Google has grown enormously over the three years in question, so the real surprise is when the new 2006 words have *reduced* in references, as is the case with **earworm**, down from 1,750,000 to 1,110,000.

grief tourist 18,000	to miswant 7,600
touch in / touch out 9,820	infomania 465,000
hand-me-ups 6,570	earworm 1,110,000
al desko 340,000	marmalade dropper 1,700
cyber slacking 60,700	me time 6,000,000

grief tourist
A person who travels to the scene of a death or murder with which they have no intimate connection. The word was coined after the death of Diana, Princess of Wales, in 1997. 7,710 mentions, when you google 'grief tourist'. See: *dark tourism*, *recreational grief*, *mourning sickness*.

touch in / touch out
Londoners using the Underground buy an 'oyster card'. They swipe the card over an electronic pad and this opens the entry gate for them. This is *touching in*. To exit their destination station, they *touch out*. 81 Google references.

hand-me-ups
'Hand-me-downs' are clothes passed from elder children to their younger siblings. *Hand-me-ups* are often items like computers, discarded by children and 'inherited' by their parents. The word dates from the 1980s and has 850 Google references.

al desko
An 'al fresco' lunch is one eaten out-of-doors. An *al desko* lunch is one eaten without leaving the office. 2,100 Google references.

cyber slacking (or **cyber loafing**)
Web-surfing or sending personal emails while you are at your office desk. 9,400 Google references.

to miswant
To want things that won't make you happy. Traceable back to an academic article in 2000. 7,100 Google references.

infomania
The state of mind of a person who pays immediate attention to all incoming emails, text messages and phone calls and who therefore gets much less done. 117,000 Google references.

earworm
A tune that goes round and round in your head, also referred to as 'stuck tune syndrome'. The 1,750,000 Google references are unreliable, as they also refer to endless varieties of real worms!

marmalade dropper (US: **muffin choker**)
A newspaper article so startling that you drop your toast and marmalade on the breakfast table. 11,600 Google references; 'Muffin choker': 10,000.

me time
Time for yourself rather than for work, the house, or the family. 1,200,000 Google references.

TV talk

Neologisms for the new reality

Cultural content

How playful and ironic new British media language, and the thinking behind it, can be. It also serves as an interesting comparison with home-culture media and language.

Preparation

Make sufficient copies of the vocabulary list opposite.

Procedure

1. Ask the students to get into small groups and elicit a definition of 'compound nouns'. Remind them that nouns can also be made up of parts of words forming a 'composite' (for example: 'docusoap' – a combination between documentary and soap opera).
2. From the list opposite, put the list of words or expressions on the board and explain that all the vocabulary comes from the world of British media, specifically relating to TV. Ask the students to guess the meanings of each item and provide reasons for their guesses. They will need to keep a written record of their answers.
3. When they have finished, elicit some answers and some of the rationales behind the guesswork – and enjoy!
4. Now hand out copies of the vocabulary list, ask the students to read them and compare their answers with those given.
5. Round off by asking whether there are any equivalents in their mother tongues.

Appointment TV
Programmes watched at their scheduled time, as opposed to watching recorded TV at a later date/time.

Bitcom
Brief sitcom-style video, accessed from the internet.

Cot potato
'Square-eyed' baby or toddler, who watches a lot of TV: a baby 'couch potato'.

Dramedy
Show or series that combines drama and comedy. Recent example: 'Desperate Housewives'.

Frankenbite
The art of switching around contestants' comments in reality TV shows to create a supposedly seamless narrative. Commonly used in 'Big Brother'.

Irritainment
Annoying but compulsive show.

Hammock
Time slot in between two popular programmes often used to introduce new shows.

Hathos
Feelings of pleasure derived from hating someone or something, like 'Big Brother' contestants.

Metal Mickey
Camera used in 'reality TV', remotely controlled, fully submersible in water, with nightvision and a 360-degree capability. Contestants cannot escape!

Mobisode
Two-minute soap opera episode created for watching on mobile phones. Early mobisodes included '24' and 'Prison Break'.

National anthems

Or are they hymns?

Cultural content

A comparison of expressions of nationhood.

Preparation

Make copies of the anthems for each student.

Procedure

1. Put the students into five groups and get each group to read one anthem and to work out the core meaning.
2. Hold a plenary so each group can report back their findings.
3. This may develop into a whole-class discussion about national anthems and their purpose. At this stage the students may well refer to their own national anthems.

Postscript

Inspiration for this activity comes from a presentation by Neil McClaren at a linguistics conference held in Jaén, Spain, in 2002: *Linguistic Patriotism: aspects of the language of some national anthems.*

Australians all let us rejoice
For we are young and free.
We've golden soil and wealth for toil,
Our home is girt by sea:
Our land abounds in nature's gifts
Of beauty rich and rare,
In history's page let every stage
Advance Australia fair,
In joyful strains then let us sing
Advance Australia fair.

My country, my country,
My country, the land of my ancestors,
My country, my nation, the nation of eternity.
With the resolve of the winds and the fire of the guns
And the determination of my nation in the land of struggle.
Palestine is my home.
Palestine is my revenge and the land of Eternity.

Land of mountains, land on the river,
Land of fields, land of cathedrals,
Land of hammers, rich into the future.
You are home to famous sons,
A people blessed with beauty,
Renowned **Austria**
Austria of high fame.

Oh **Belgium**, beloved mother,
Our hearts are yours, our arms are yours,
Our blood is yours, oh Motherland.
You will live on, we swear it,
You will live for ever, great and beautiful.
And your invincible unity
Will bear this immortal emblem:
King, Law and Liberty
King, Law and Liberty
King, Law and Liberty.

As long as deep in the heart
The soul of a Jew yearns,
And forward to the East
To **Zion**, the eye looks,
Our hope will not be lost,
The hope of two thousand years,
To be a free nation in our land,
The land of Zion and Jerusalem.

Chapter Three

Frames for studying culture

When you enter a foreign culture you tend to notice environmental and behavioural things. But behind most of these phenomena (these appearances) you will discover cultural beliefs. It is absolutely normal to haggle for products in Middle Eastern and North African markets. The haggling might seem quite fierce and combative, but both parties enter into the process with gusto, each believing that they will both eventually get what they want from the transaction. It is a long way from the fixed pricing of Western supermarkets.

Chapter Three offers you a series of mental filters, or thinking frames, for presenting 'cultural content' in the classroom, providing a bundle of useful and eminently practical tools for understanding culture that will help your students to become more aware of cultural diversity.

On course!

Secret agendas, shared surveys

Cultural content

Choosing course or class content can be student-active.

Preparation

Prepare at least one comment for each element of the content you intend to cover. Have at least 20 'conversational' sentences/topics – there are some examples below for you.

Put each one on a separate piece of paper, place each set in an envelope, one envelope per group. Also have enough uncut sentence sheets for everyone.

Procedure

1. Ask the students how they decide what to talk about in conversations and how topics change during a conversation. You need to elicit that participants in conversations change topics so that they get to talk about the things they want – the things 'on their agenda'.
2. Put the students into small groups and hand out the envelopes, asking each group member to take out three or four sentences. Each student should read their own sentences silently but *not* show them to anyone. If there are comprehension problems, deal with these individually and privately.
3. Their sentences are their 'secret agenda' for the conversation. Nobody has the same agenda and the object of the activity is to gently guide the conversation so that each person can say their sentences, or something very close, without the rest of the group realising.
4. Model the activity with a student. You manipulate the conversation, and the class helps your volunteer to identify your target sentence.
5. Let the activity commence! Tell the students they are at a conference to discuss aspects of the target culture. Give them a starting topic – immigration or education, etc. Each time they manage to place one of their sentences they get a point and move on to another one. The winner is the student with the most points.
6. End the activity once all the sentences have been used, or when it feels right.
7. Finally, hand out the whole sentence sheet to the students. They mark each sentence:
   - Not important
   - Important
   - Very important

   Use their shared judgements of relevance to structure your course, to revise content – or simply to generate individual lesson discussion activity.

Postscript

We learned this mechanism from Maley and Duff's *Drama Techniques in Language Learning*, CUP, 1978.

- Have you heard about Estuary English? Apparently, most kids in Southern England speak it these days!
- What do you think of the Prime Minister?
- What is the favourite British dish?
- What do you imagine when you think of British pub culture?
- What is the preferred shopping experience for most Britons – the High Street or the mall?
- What do you see as the main differences between British and your societies?
- I think privatisation of public utilities has changed the face of British society forever.
- A lot of British people are talking about the 'New Royals' and 'sacking the Royal family'. What's your opinion?
- The British are shopaholics!
- British cuisine has been much maligned. It now ranks amongst the best in Europe.
- Britain is, allegedly, multicultural and multi-ethnic. I wonder if the various ethnic groups feel part of the whole or very separate entities.
- Britain's new class system was based on 'profession'.
- What do you think the average Briton thinks about the asylum seekers who now live in the UK?
- What do your compatriots think about the British in general?
- Do you know that in the last 30 years the average female dress size has gone up from a 38 to a 44?
- The British government is quite worried that children are going to be obese. Already lots of adults are.
- There is a growing 'couch potato' culture – people sitting watching TV, eating junk food – with no exercise at all.
- How are British families different from yours?
- Do you and the British bring up your children differently?
- How do British leisure activities differ from yours?

Onion ring culture

Differences go deep

Cultural content

Students see the relationships between the products of culture and the values behind them.

Preparation

It is a good idea to do this activity yourself first, so you are prepared for some of the things that might come up.

Procedure

1. Ask the students (in pairs or small groups) to prepare a list of all the things they think would come under the heading of 'culture'. When everyone is ready, let them compare their findings. You might want to do some feedback in plenary.
2. Ask them to think of a list of things they think would *not* come under the heading of 'culture'. (This list will probably be much smaller!)

   Again, allow the groups to compare notes. (For example: weather, of itself, is not part of culture, but how we live with it is.)
3. Ask the students to close their eyes and visualise getting off a plane or boat and entering a very different country to their own. (They may draw on memory or on their imagination.) They should imagine the temperature, sounds, smells, etc, of this new place.
4. When they are ready, ask them to imagine a journey around a town in this new place. (This could be on foot, by taxi, or any local form of transport.) They should take in all the new sights, sounds, smells, etc, and build up a strong impression of the place.

   While they are doing this, draw four concentric circles on the board (see the diagram opposite). In the innermost circle, write 'Core beliefs'.
5. When the students are ready, tell them to list the things they noticed which were different from their own countries.

   Ask them to give you some of their ideas. (You might get items like: architecture, height of buildings, street food, language, body language, money, clothes, etc.) Write these in the outer circle on the board. Explain that these things are 'products' of a culture and are the things we tend to notice when they differ from our own.
6. Now ask the students to imagine or remember learning a bit more about the country, having met a few people and stayed there for a week or so. What did they learn about the new country? Ask them to make lists and compare notes with those working close by.
7. While they are doing this, label the other sections in the 'onion ring': 'Rituals and practices' (closest to the centre) and 'Icons' (on the inside of 'Products').
   - An example of rituals/practice is the game of football, with all its rules and regulations, kit, officials, supporters, etc.
   - Icons or figureheads for this practice might be Maradona, Pele, Messi or Beckham.
8. When the students are ready, invite them to put their ideas in the relevant places in your onion ring.
9. Through plenary discussion, make any adjustments to the placing of these practices, rituals or icons.

   You may be able to draw several lines through the onion ring from *belief* to *product*, showing in a powerful way that when we sneer at seemingly small things – cultural products of another country – the criticism goes a lot deeper than we think. As, of course, does the praise!

Postscript

The simplified onion ring diagram is adapted from Trompenaars. (See Part A, on page 10, for more information.)

Onion ring diagram

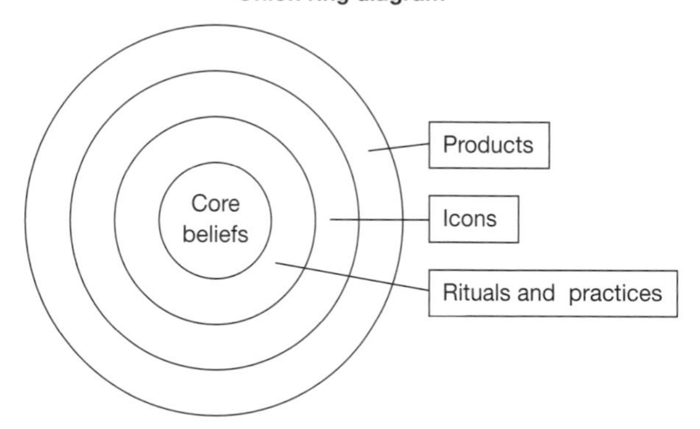

Cultural concepts

What is this culture thing, anyway?

Cultural content

A forum where students can explore the philosophical nature of culture.

Procedure

1. Write these questions on the board:
   - Is any one culture simpler, better or worse than others? What is the evidence for your view?
   - What is the most important thing *your* culture has given to the world?
   - When people from other countries think about your culture, what do they normally think of? What are some of the things they may wonder about?
2. Group the students in fours and get them to choose a question and discuss it. They have ten minutes.
3. Ask each group to report on their discussions.

Postscript

Below is an extensive list of further philosophical questions. You can choose to use these at the beginning of a course, to gauge students' awareness, or indeed later on.

All the issues raised in this activity were given to us by a much-loved Pilgrims colleague (who wishes to remain anonymous).

- How would you describe culture? What are some of the things culture consists of?
- What do you think people typically consider as culture? How limited do you think this view is?
- How do different beliefs, ethics or values influence people's behaviours and the society they live in? What factors can you think of that shape one's world view, values and beliefs?
- How does culture reveal itself in a society? What are some of the ways or channels through which culture can be characterised, practised and reproduced?
- Does culture show discrepancies across geographical regions, nations, countries, and so forth? If yes, why, and how so? Are there also universal qualities between people of different cultures?
- What are some of the potential conflicts that are likely to occur due to lack of knowledge of the cultural differences when people of different cultures and norms meet up?
- What safety measures can be taken to prevent or reduce cultural misunderstandings and clashes and their potential negative effects?
- Can you think of ways of how one would discover and gain knowledge of others' cultures? What would you do if you did learn about another culture?
- If a group of people came to your country from overseas, what advice would you give them? What do you think would surprise them? How do you think they would feel during their stay in your country?
- What are some of the practices associated with your own culture? Do you find them all appealing, or are there things that you are not fond of about your culture?
- What is the best/most important thing you think your culture/country has adopted from another culture?
- What would you like to know about a different culture before you travelled to a different country? How would you feel if you left your home culture and entered into a completely new culture?
- What do we mean when we say 'When in Rome, do as the Romans do'? Do you think it is always good advice? Why, or why not? Can you remember any other idioms or expressions about culture?
- How is language related to culture? Why would one need to learn about the culture of the native speakers of a language being studied?
- Have you searched for any information regarding native English speakers' cultures through books, the internet, or other sources? What did you discover? In what ways were they alike or different from those of your own culture? What would you like to know about their culture that you have not explored yet?
- Would you ever consider marrying a native speaker of English, or living permanently in an English-speaking country?
  - If yes, why?
  - If no, why not?

  If you would, how would intercultural awareness and cultural acceptance play a role in your experiences?

This is my life!

Arranged marriages versus love marriages

Cultural content

A debate where students explore the contentious nature of cultural contrasts.

Procedure

1. Put the students into groups of eight. Assign pairs within each group (two As, two Bs, two Cs and two Ds).
2. Tell the pairs that they have seven minutes to prepare their arguments for a debate on marriage. They may make brief notes.
   - The As prepare as many arguments as possible in favour of love marriages.
   - The Bs prepare as many arguments as possible against love marriages.
   - The Cs prepare as many arguments as possible in favour of arranged marriages.
   - The Ds prepare as many arguments as possible against arranged marriages.

   Explain that it does not matter what the students' real beliefs may be: they are to act like lawyers defending a brief. Time the seven minutes.
3. Now tell each pair to pick *one* of their arguments and spend two minutes preparing to present it to the rest of their group of eight. Only one from each pair will speak. They will have to speak for 30 seconds. Time the two-minute preparation time.
4. They now give their 30-second, timed speeches: first an A, then a B, then a C, then a D. You will call time to the whole class, so that all the As speak, then the Bs, etc, at the same time in their different groups.
5. Finally, get the groups to tell each other what they *really* think about the issue!
6. If appropriate, ask your students to write you an essay or letter about arranged marriages.

Postscript

We learnt this 'critical thinking' activity type from *Global Issues* by Sampedro and Hillyard, OUP, 2004. You can use it with any contentious cultural issue such as: wearing the hijab, faith schools, or the rights and wrongs of the death penalty.

Culture statues

Freeze, please!

Cultural content

Students experience concepts through their bodies.

Procedure

1. Write up on the board the list of cultural keywords below.
2. Group the students in sixes and tell them they are to choose one keyword they feel they understand.
3. They will then have ten minutes to organise themselves into a group statue that represents the concept they have chosen. Tell them they will have to 'freeze' their *tableau vivant* and stay steady and motionless for some 20 seconds.
4. Ask the groups to show the others their statues and to hold each statue for 20 seconds.
5. Allow time for the students to comment on the 'fit' between each statue and the cultural keyword.

Postscript

You can use this activity for getting students to experience keywords for the cultures of the UK, US, Canada, Ghana, India, etc. 'Tableaux vivants' are also powerful in getting students to explore ideas that are key in their own home cultures.

This list of cultural keywords was proposed by Kate Fox in *Watching the English – The Hidden Rules of English Behaviour*, Hodder and Stoughton, 2004.

(Eeyore, the donkey, is a glum, self-pitying, complaining character in A A Milne's *Winnie the Pooh* books.)

humour	moderation
hypocrisy	modesty
empiricism	eeyorishness
fair play	courtesy
class consciousness	

My values, your culture

A respectful roleplay

Cultural content

To contrast values learned in the home culture from a significant elder (a teacher, family member, etc) with the way of life in the target culture.

Preparation

Make copies of the texts opposite, told by a young, male, Afghani student, now living in the UK and by a female teacher.

Procedure

1. Share the texts opposite with your students, requesting that they think about them. Explain that the class is going to discuss a problem noticed by a UK female teacher concerning one of her students.
2. Ask them to work in two groups. Group A should take the role of the teacher and Group B the Afghani boy. Each group should work out a strategy for explaining the problem to the other group in a respectful way.

   You might need to elicit the crux of the matter (the nature of respect for each of the two cultures) before the discussion begins. Remember: in this situation neither party would wish to offend the other.
3. When they are ready, pair the students off (one from Group A and one from Group B) and begin to roleplay the problem, noting if voices are raised or if the discussion gets too confrontational.
4. When it feels right, stop the activity and ask the students to get back into their original groups. They should then discuss how they felt: being judged and having their judgement questioned so openly.
5. In plenary, elicit their comments.

Postscript

This activity may be best suited to classes containing refugee/ immigrant participants, who may come from very different cultures with very different values. It can be an interesting starting point from which to analyse the target culture.

The feedback session might raise a lot of issues the students have been mulling over for a while. If you feel able to deal with these, fine. If not, you could bring the discussion back to the individuals in the story and what the problems were with their individual notions of respect.

The 'key worker' referred to by the student is someone working for Social Services, who has a special responsibility for the care of people like the boy in this story.

The student

In our mosque we had a very kind and wise teacher. He taught us the Koran and gave us advice on how to be good Muslims. I remember him teaching us about respect. He explained that our women were precious and that we must always protect them and respect them. I knew this was one of his most important lessons. I was sometimes naughty to my sisters but I tried very hard to think about what our imam said. Before I left Afghanistan, my mother said I was a good boy and a good Muslim.

Here, your sons do not respect or protect their women. I see the mothers out in the street. Sometimes they smoke in the street where everyone can see, their clothes are not modest and their sons do not care – sometimes they are not polite to their mothers.

I do not have my mother here, but I try to behave respectfully, especially to my key worker and my teachers, but now it is summer they do not wear modest clothes. It is hard for me to respect them because I think they don't respect themselves.

The teacher

In class the boy does not look at me and, recently, has not answered questions I have put to him. His homework is fine, but I am worried that something is wrong. I feel he has stopped behaving respectfully towards me, but I don't know why.

Culture words

Where do they belong?

Cultural content

Students discover what 'culture' is about, in their view.

Preparation

Do the following activity yourself first, in order to be ready to help your students.

Draw five concentric circles and in the middle of the inner circle write the word 'bird'. Now place these birds:

chaffinch, bat, eagle, hen, seagull, ostrich

If you think that the word is not very 'birdy', put it in one of the outer circles. If you think it is 'very birdy', put it near the centre. Many people would put 'bat' outside the circle, as it is a mammal. They would put an ostrich in an outer circle as it can't fly. The theory is that a member of a set can belong to this set with varying degrees of completeness.

Have sufficient sheets of A4 paper for each student.

Procedure

1. Ask the students student to draw five concentric circles on a clean sheet of paper. Tell them to make the circles fill the paper. In the middle, they write the word *Culture*.
2. Explain that some ideas/words may belong very strongly to the '*culture* set' while others are either outside it or belong much more weakly. You might want to use the 'bird' example to illustrate your point.
3. Draw the concentric circles on the board yourself, placing 'Culture' in the centre.
4. Give the students the term 'individualism' and ask them where they think it goes in the circles. Then give them 'clothes pegs' and ask them to place this, too.
5. Explain that you will give them words and that they are to place them, according to their own criteria, in *their* circles, depending on how strongly they belong to the 'culture' area.
6. If you think they don't know these words, either explain or translate them. Then slowly dictate the words opposite.
7. Group the students in fours and ask them to explain their placing of the words to each other.
8. Finally, ask the students to come and write on the board the four words or expressions they put nearest the centre – and finish with a general discussion.

implicit rules	smile
we/they	law
to bow	ostracism
politeness	flat roof
time	voting
minus 25 degrees	toilet
courtship	fork
anger	island
directness	poverty
weather forecast	snow-line
inclusion	insights
pigsty	distance
retro-culture shock	netiquette
barmitzva	breakdown
ring	compulsion
aubergine	belief
seaweed	

Postscript

This is an application of Prototype Theory, which we first learnt from Jean Aitchison's *Good Birds, Better Birds and Amazing Birds*, Vocabulary in Applied Linguistics, 1992.

Icebergs

Things may be hidden but they're still there

Cultural content

A framework to increase awareness of cultural stereotyping and facilitate genuine discussion on 'cultural myth versus cultural reality'.

Procedure

1. Ask a volunteer to draw an iceberg on the board and get the students to copy it onto two sheets of A4 paper. Point out that most of the iceberg is hidden under the water:
   - In the same way that people know things about the UK and this will be the visible part of the iceberg, there are many things that will not be at all obvious to 'outsiders'.
   - For example, many people don't know that British cuisine is now ranked very highly in the gastronomic world.
2. Ask the students to fill in one of their icebergs, putting information both above the water line (things they think people *will know* about their country) and below (things they think people *won't know* about their country).
3. Pair the students so that they will be working with a partner from a different country, or region of the same country, if possible. Ask them to think about the country/region *of their partner*. Get them to fill the 'above water' section of the other iceberg with information they know about this country/region. They should fill in the 'below water' section with guesses and questions.
4. Now ask the pairs to exchange papers and read them to see if their guesses were correct or their questions answered. Ask them to talk about any issues raised.
5. As a whole-class activity, elicit feedback around 'Things that surprised you or differences/similarities you found'.

Variations

This is an extremely powerful framework with numerous possible areas for its use:

- Get the students to answer the questions 'How I fit my culture and how I don't' or 'What I like about my culture and what I don't'.
- Get a group of students to speculate about you, their teacher! (The students fill in the iceberg in small groups, then, collectively, add the information/questions/guesses they want to keep to the 'final draft'. You will also need to fill in a sheet about yourself.)
- Get exchange students thinking about their new schools, partners, families and all the related 'rules'.

Postscript

This activity idea came from Mary Alice Soriero de Martínez.

Our house

There's room for reflection

Cultural content

An exploration of students' personal understanding of what 'house' means, as well as its cultural meanings within their communities.

Procedure

1. Group the students in fours to discuss which they feel to be the most important room in their house.
2. Tell them to get up, move around the room, find a partner who has decided on the same room and sit down together. Both take paper and pen and, before starting to write, the partners move apart so they can't talk to each other.
   - Person A in the pair takes on the role of the house, and in this role writes a three-paragraph letter to the room they have both chosen. The letter starts:
     Dear Room,
   - Person B takes on the role of the room chosen and writes a three-paragraph letter to the house. The letter starts:
     Dear House,
3. When the students have mostly finished writing, ask them to exchange letters, return to their writing places and answer the letter they have just received from their partner.
4. Bring the pairs together to exchange their answers, read them and comment on the correspondence.
5. Finally, bring the pairs together into groups of six (a good number to get a variety of opinion) to discuss what each person has learnt about the concept of house from all that has been written and said.

Postscript

The technique of the 'whole' writing to the 'part', and vice-versa can be usefully used to explore other areas of culture. For example:

- *The community* writes to the *teenager*, and vice-versa.
- *The class system* writes to the UK *lower middle class*, and vice-versa.

Four-way states of mind

Different ways of perceiving differences

Cultural content

Students make their attitudes towards the beliefs and behaviours of another culture explicit and conscious.

Preparation

Look at the four attitudes to cultural difference in Mario's examples below, to help you explain them, but use examples *of your own* with your students. Your own examples will be much more useful to your class than ours.

Remember: the four states of mind are intended as descriptive frames. There is no feeling that one state of mind is 'better' or 'morally superior' to another.

Procedure

1. Tell the class of a time when your state of mind was 'Upward evolutionist':
   - **Upward evolutionist** – *looking up to*

   If appropriate, give further examples – colonised people tend to have this attitude towards the colonising culture.
2. Ask the students to work in fours and come up with times when they felt this way towards the mindset and behaviours of another cultural group in their country or abroad. It could be a different cultural sub-group within their extended family.
3. Discuss some of the ideas as a whole-class activity.
4. Follow the steps above, working on the other three cultural states of mind, starting off with your own personal examples each time:
   - **Downward evolutionist** – *looking down on*
   - **Universalist** – *sameness*
   - **Relativist** – *both OK*
5. Round off the lesson by getting answers from the whole class to this question:

   What is the most interesting thing you have found out about yourself in this lesson?

Postscript

We met the above thinking/feeling frame in the work of Richard Shweder. There's more information in Part A on page 11.

Upward evolutionist state of mind

- Mario writes: *I admire the way Italians, Maltese, Greeks and Spanish people cook, with plenty of simple vegetables, pasta and olive oil. I admire their sense of timing and the idea of 'slow food' and of sitting round a table chatting.*
- Mario feels that the Northern Mediterranean way of cooking and 'meal socialising' is superior to the way his English compatriots live in this area. The state of mind is admiration.

Downward evolutionist state of mind

- Mario writes: *Many 30 year olds in the UK cover their garden with lawn and have a wooden deck near the house. They grow no flowers or vegetables. My 39-year-old son does this and I feel a gardener's contempt for him in this. Yes, I look down on his way of using his garden.*
- Mario feels his culture in this area of gardening is superior to his son's. He feels negative about many of the next generation's way of using garden space. The state of mind is contempt.

Universalist state of mind

- Mario writes: *The term 'teacher' designates a huge number of different roles. A form teacher in Japan has to fix job interviews for school leavers while a Gymnasium teacher in Germany deals with the student within the parameters of the subject. Each society defines the role and duties of the teacher.*
- Mario thinks that, despite these marked role differences, there are common features that apply to all teachers in all societies. All teachers stand *in loco parentis* for a large part of the day and share the task of transmitting knowledge, behaviours and beliefs – there is fundamental sameness in the meaning of the word 'teacher'.

Relativist state of mind

- Mario writes: *In a shop in Italy, I place my money in the money container on the counter between the assistant and me. In the UK, I put money onto the assistant's hand.*
- Mario says his state of mind is relativist as he can produce either behaviour in the correct cultural setting. Switching behaviours here costs him nothing. The state of mind is similar to bi-lingualism: both money behaviours feel appropriate, good and comfortable in their contexts.

Talking and turn taking

In Japan they have a word for it

Cultural content

Students are made aware of the way their mother-tongue discourse patterns are particular and non-universal – and that the same is true of English.

Procedure

1. Pair the students and ask each pair to decide who is A and who is B.
2. Take the B students out of the classroom and tell them they are to do the following things when they go back to their partner:
   - They will ask their partner to suggest what they should both talk about for three minutes.
   - After everything their partner says, they need to add an agreement-seeking question tag. For example:
     - *You don't like Madonna, do you?*
     - *The weather's great today, isn't it?*
3. The B students go back into the classroom and have a 3-minute, agreement-seeking dialogue with their A partner.

   When they have finished, ask the As round the room how they felt about the way their B person was behaving. Listen to different contributions, but don't say anything yet.
4. Now the Bs stay in the classroom and you take the As out. Tell the As to choose a topic of conversation and, when they go back in, let their partner know what it is. The moment their partner says something, they are to interrupt and hold the floor for as long as they can. Tell them the conversation will last five minutes and that you will time it.
5. Time the conversations and then ask the Bs to describe how the As were behaving and how they felt about it. Listen to different contributions, but don't say anything yet.
6. Now tell the students they are going to do one more activity. They change partners.

   The As should prepare to question the Bs about whatever they feel like. Take the Bs outside. Tell them they must count to three, mentally, before answering A's questions. They then give the shortest possible answer. The best answers are one-word utterances. The Bs go back in and assume this minimalist style of talking.

   The As feed back their feelings.
7. Put the students in groups of four to six to compare the three conversational styles they have been playing with and to comment on how they differ from the conversation style of their mother tongues. At this point, you might explain the information in the box below. Do any of the students know someone who speaks in one of these ways?
8. Finally, ask the students which cultural features strike them in the varieties of English they are exposed to.

Postscript

What you have in this activity is one salient feature picked from what could be considered typical Japanese discourse (*aizuchi*), typical Greek male discourse and typical Finnish discourse, all exaggerated so as to make it very obvious and visible to students who do not know these culture-governed ways of speaking.

Conversational styles

Agreement seeking

Seeks harmony. The Japanese have a word for this style of conversation: *aizuchi*.

Holding the floor

Involves ensuring that it is you who is doing the most speaking. This conversational feature is not uncommon in Greece, more especially among male speakers.

Minimalist

Values listening more than speaking. Succinctness and brevity are appreciated. In Finland, for example, there is an expression: *You have one mouth and two ears; use them in that proportion.*

Time is of the essence

Is my late your early?

Cultural content

Students are made aware of the difference between the time conventions in their countries compared with, for example, middle-class Canadian time conventions.

Preparation

Make copies of the Canadian quantification text opposite, one for each student.

Procedure

1. Explain to the students that you are going to dictate a number of sentences and that they should write these down and also write down a 'quantification'. For example:

   If the sentence you dictate is *'She got up early on Tuesday morning'*, the students write this and also jot down what they consider to be 'early' as a getting-up time on a Tuesday morning in their culture.

2. Dictate the list of sentences opposite, without the Canadian quantifications. After the first one, remind them to quantify.
3. When the students have finished, ask them to compare their quantifications and then give out the Canadian quantification sheets.
4. Ask them to check any spelling mistakes they have made in their taking down of the sentences and look at the times.
5. Round off with any comments they want to make about similarities or differences.

Variation

Write the names of the months up on the board and ask the students to copy them out and write down against each:

- the normal temperature for the month
- the normal humidity
- two weather features they associate with the month: *rain, snow, fog, light winds*, etc

In a multi-national class, this can lead to a new awareness of other people's climates.

Postscript

The Canadian times were suggested by Lindsay Clandfield. We learnt the quantification dictation idea from Paul Davis's book, *Dictation Many Ways*, CUP, 1989.

	Canadian quantifications
She got up early on Tuesday morning, a workday.	**between 5.00 and 6.00**
The traffic was heavy and it took her a long time to get to work.	**over an hour**
She arrived at work on time.	**9.00 am**
She took a normal length of time for her lunch break.	**one hour**
He got back home very late from work.	**after 7.00**
They had dinner rather late.	**after 7.00**
That weekend they had lunch at the normal sort of time.	**one-ish**
They were invited to supper with friends who like eating early.	**before 7.00**
They were invited for a specific time but, as they were polite, they arrived at the time their hosts *expected* they would.	**between 10 and 20 minutes late**
They got home and watched the last national TV news.	**from 10.00 to 10.30**
As the next day was a workday, they went to bed at a sensible time.	**around eleven-ish**
They usually put their 8 year old to bed fairly early as he has to get to school by the right time next morning. (Two quantifications here)	**a bit before 9.00 pm / 8.45 am**
Occasionally the 8 year old gets to stay up really late.	**11.00 pm or even midnight**

Culture construction

Your very own society

Cultural content

Students construct and respond to new cultures of their own creation.

Preparation

None, although it is a good idea to have done the *Onion ring culture* activity first (see page 53).

Procedure

1. Divide the class into groups of six to eight. They will need to work in some privacy, so organise the space accordingly – perhaps you can use the classroom and an outside space, or two rooms.
2. Tell the students that they are going to invent their own society. This society has its own country and has complex systems of hierarchy, behaviour, etiquette and values. It will be up to each group to decide what these are.
3. To get them started, ask the students to decide on how people in their new culture greet each other and strangers, how they show respect, how they show coldness and distance, etc.
4. Make sure each group knows what to do. Stress that the activity is supposed to be fun and they shouldn't censor their initial ideas but offer them up for discussion in their groups.
5. Monitor them closely, offering suggestions to keep them going. You might like to get them thinking about things like the following:
   - Who has status in society and who doesn't (and how they can show this)?
   - How do they show disapproval, enthusiasm, polite interest, agreement/disagreement?

   They will need about 30 minutes for this part of the activity.
6. Tell each group they are going to meet some very strange cultures and that they should try and find out as much as they can about each of them, noting any 'odd behaviour' they come across.

   Now get the cultures to meet. You could 'host' a diplomatic reception. This is usually a hilarious event!
7. When the activity seems to have come to a natural close, get the groups to compare notes on what they noticed. For example:
   - the way they/others reacted (in role in their invented cultures, of course) when someone 'did something wrong'
   - the way they themselves behaved when finding out about other cultures
   - their impressions of the other cultures they met – their behaviours/beliefs
8. Finally, conduct feedback in one of the following ways:
   - Divide the groups in half. One half stays put and the rest move to the group on their right. They give/receive feedback on how it felt to meet the new cultures and find out the reasons for some of the odd behaviours they noticed. After a few minutes move them on so that everyone gets/gives some feedback. Finally, do a whole-class feedback.
   - Divide the board into as many columns as you have 'cultures'. Ask your students to write observations about the cultures they met, *not* the one they invented. Then ask the groups to stand by their 'home culture' and give the class feedback on the comments written.
   - Conduct whole-class feedback, perhaps using the 'onion ring' model to map behaviours. You could also look at Shweder's four ways of responding to cultures (see page 11 in Part A).

A mind map of Europe

Geographical location or cultural artifice?

Cultural content

'Europe' may be more of a cultural construct than a geographical continent.

Preparation

Have photocopies of a map of the world for each student.

Procedure

1. Hand out the photocopied maps. Ask the students to work individually and write a capital 'E' in each country that *they personally* regard to be part of Europe.
2. Ask them to move into groups of four or five and compare their answers. Where there is disagreement, ask them to justify their answers. Hold a plenary feedback and highlight 'contentious countries' on the board.
3. Show the first extract below on an OHP transparency or on the board and ask the students to discuss in small groups what these European *values* might be. Hold another plenary feedback and pool the ideas on the board.
4. Now show a further extract from this same article articulating these values and compare these values with those pooled on the board.
5. Discuss the differences and ask the students if they think the countries they marked with 'E', including the contentious ones, conform to the above values.
6. Finally, open up a discussion as to whether the students agree with the writer's view that 'maps are defined in minds'. Here are some points you might like to include:
   - Israel, Ukraine and Turkey can enter football teams into the European Champions League.
   - Israel takes part in the Eurovision Song Contest.
   - There were Muslims a) In the old Soviet Union before it broke up and b) in Yugoslavia before the Serbo-Croat war.

Postscript

This activity was given to us by a Pilgrims colleague and the extracts are taken from 'Values Define Europe, Not Borders' by Olli Rehn, *Financial Times*, 4th January, 2005.

> **1** I am often asked where Europe's ultimate borders lie. My answer is that the map of Europe is defined in the minds of Europeans. Geography sets the frame, but fundamentally it is values that make the borders of Europe.
>
> **2** ... the most fundamental [values] ... are liberty and solidarity, tolerance and human rights, democracy and the rule of law.

The question of health

A question of faith?

Cultural content

Using one African-English-speaking mindset to examine the role of Western 'scientific' medicine.

Procedure

1. Write this up on the board:
   - *Traditional healers provide safe health for the people of Africa.*
   - *About 85% of the general population in Africa rely on the traditional, natural forms of health care we provide.*
2. Group the students in fours (as heterogeneously as possible, if this is a culturally-mixed class). Ask them to discuss how much illness provokes recourse to a Western medically-trained doctor and how much to other health carers (acupuncturists, Bach remedy practitioners, traditional Chinese medicators, shamans, etc).
3. Dictate the text below to a student scribe at the board and ask each student to write a two-paragraph reaction to the text; then group them again in fours to read each other's texts.
4. Put the students into two groups: 'natural medicine' and 'pharmaceutical medicine'. Explain that in the English debating tradition, they do not have to believe in the side they are supporting.
5. Ask each group to come up with a list of advantages of their kind of medicine, which they will use to present their case to the other group. At this stage, go round, suggesting vocabulary and asking questions to help.
6. Get the students to present their arguments and then debate the issue in plenary, rounding off with a vote – according to their conscience.

Postscript

The two quotes above are taken from a Traditional Healers' Organization advertisement in the *Mail and Guardian* newspaper, South Africa, 24th December, 2004.

> For more than a century the pharmaceutical industry has discredited and faulted traditional natural medicine in order to provoke their multi-million investment business with patented drugs.
>
> But now the fatal side-effects of prescription drugs have become the hallmark of modern, pharmaceutical-based medicine. In the industrialised world, the epidemic of deadly side-effects of these drugs has become the third largest cause of death.

Codes of conduct

Driving me crazy

Cultural content

Exploring and explaining different codes of behaviour in everyday situations.

Preparation

Prepare a copy of the 'driving rules' texts for each student.

Procedure

1. Hand out the text 'Re-active rules'. Ask the students to imagine they are the writer of this text.
   What could have happened to this person in order for these rules to be learned?
2. Ask them to share their ideas and then explain the background for the text:
   'I have been driving for 20 years. Recently, I travelled to a country where many of my ideas of polite road behaviour were turned upside-down. The rules I learned from this experience may not be absolutely true – they are simply what I internalised.'
3. Now tell the students to imagine they are driving instructors in the country concerned. It is their job to write a new list of rules and the rationale for them. The finished product is intended as a handout to be given to foreign tourists by car-hire companies. Get the students working in groups so they can collaborate.
4. Display the finished texts for everybody to read.
5. Hand out the 'answer sheet' – the 'Pro-active' rules written by a driver from the country concerned – so that the students can compare it with their own rationales.
6. In small groups, ask the students to share how they felt about the new culture:
   - while reading about these 'rules'
   - as driving instructors 'explaining' their rules
7. Finally, in plenary, having heard the rationale for these rules, how do they see the culture now?

Re-active rules

1. Speed limits are irrelevant. Drive as fast as you possibly can and if you go slower than the rest of the traffic, expect to be given a hard time.
2. On main roads and motorways, imagine you are on a race track and drive accordingly, even though you will probably be on a single or, at best, dual carriageway.
3. Unless there is a pedestrian crossing with traffic lights that are *red*, or you are going very slowly due to traffic congestion, ignore pedestrians. Roads belong to cars. If you stop for a pedestrian for no good reason, your ears will be assaulted by the horns of the drivers behind you.
4. When a car comes speeding up behind you, pull onto the hard shoulder to let it pass. You will be rewarded by a flash of lights as the car speeds away. If not, you will find the rear of your car being nosed by the car behind, horn blaring and driver very angry.
5. When a driver pulls out in front of you, causing you to screech to a halt, sweating with fear, do not shout at or pursue the driver. Often they are armed and if you are not, it is unwise to argue.
6. Taxi-buses, usually vans, really do own the road. As road owners, they don't feel the need to indicate if they want to pull out onto the road or stop suddenly to pick up passengers. You should never argue with the drivers. They too are sometimes armed and have a reputation for violence. Also, the taxi-buses are often full of busy people trying to get somewhere and they won't like it if you hold them up.

Pro-active rules

1. Speed limits are guidelines. Obviously you can't speed in bad weather conditions unless you have a clear road. We know what we are doing and we use our judgement.
2. It is true that our roads must seem fast to you, but then you all do what you're told – fair play and obeying rules, and all that. We want to get to places. We don't want to admire the view.
3. Pedestrians generally cross a road when the road is clear. In built-up areas the traffic gets stuck, anyway, so they can cross. At big intersections cars must stop for traffic lights, so pedestrians can cross there, too.
4. If you are going too slowly for the driver behind you, you must let him pass. If he has to go across the central line of the road, he is in danger from oncoming traffic. If you pull over to the side of the road, the hard shoulder, no-one is in danger.
5. If a driver thinks he can get into the road in time, he probably will. It is very unusual for a man to pull a gun on a woman unless he wants her car or what's in it. You mustn't think that men go round with guns to point at people just because they don't like their attitude.
6. You must be careful about the taxis. They are OK, but it's best if you keep them at a safe distance. If you can't do this, then keep your clutch and brake covered – just in case.

Walk on the wild side

Is street violence everywhere?

Cultural content

Students reflect on violence in the streets and the reasons for it.

Preparation

Have ready an OHT of the information you wish to share. Prepare printed copies if you prefer.

Procedure

1. Dictate the following quote and ask the students to discuss it in pairs and what they understand by it. Hold some whole-class feedback.

   As long as there is unsliced bread, opportunities for knife crime will exist. [1]

2. Display the information in the first box opposite [2] on the OHP or hand it out, and ask the class if there is anything here that particularly surprises or interests them.
3. The students work in groups to brainstorm the main motivations for knife crime. Pool the results on the board.
4. Display or distribute the comments in the second box opposite for the groups to compare with the reasons they have just brainstormed and compare these with the five main motives [3] people have given for their attacks:
   - To have a good time
   - To show off
   - For the buzz
   - A desire to fight
   - Informal justice
5. Ask the students (in pairs or small groups) to talk about knife crime in their own countries.
   - Are the reasons above the same?
   - Are there any other factors?
6. Finally, they bring their conclusions to plenary.

Postscript

[1] 'Knife crime': a review for *Centre for Crime and Justice Studies*, August 2006.

[2] The statistics quoted are from a BBC online article, *Muggers commit crimes 'for kicks'*, 29th November 2006.

[3] The five motives are adapted from a study funded by the Economic and Social Research Council, cited in *The Times* newspaper, 30th November 2006.

- Attacks in which a knife was used during mugging rose by 73% in the UK between 2005/2006.
- There was an increase of 55% in random knife attacks on strangers during the same time period.
- The 2005 'knife amnesty' (where people were allowed to hand in knives without being prosecuted) and increasing sentence length for carrying knives does not appear to have helped in any significant way.
- The decade preceding 2005 had seen a decline in knife carrying.
- One third of schoolchildren claim to have carried a knife at some time in the past year.
- The percentage of knife carriers in children excluded from school is 57%.
- Many young people say they carry a knife as a means of protection.

To have a good time

I went to the pub, partied the money away and then the next day I got arrested.

To show off

After we'd done a few armed robberies I bought a brand new car, I love cars … I just love cars … I like clothes and having a good time. It's like showing off, really.

For the buzz

It wasn't even for money, I had money. It was more like the buzz you get from doing things. It wasn't like for money – I was more addicted to robbing than I was to drugs. Just get a funny feeling when I go out robbing.

A desire to fight

I started to try to make my way home but I had spent a lot of money on drink. I picked a fight with someone on the street. They were the first people I came across …

Informal justice

This guy owed my mate a thousand pounds of rent … I saw him get three hundred quid out of the bank and I said to him give my mate a hundred and fifty quid, you know.

Buy now, pay later!

'Neither a borrower nor a lender be'

Cultural content

Students look at attitudes to borrowing in the UK in order to be more aware of how their cultures deal with debt.

Procedure

1. Ask each student to write down three occasions when they have *lent* money or goods – and three occasions when they have *borrowed*. Then group them in fours to discuss how they feel about borrowing and lending.
2. Dictate the sentences in the first box opposite to the groups and ask the students to check their understanding of the ideas. Explain as necessary. For example:
   - what the term 'Briton' covers
   - mortgages on houses
   - an unsecured loan
   - the Citizens Advice Bureau
   - student tuition fees
   - student loans
3. In their fours, they discuss whether the borrowing situation is the same or different in their country.
4. Now read the passage in the second box to the students and ask them to jot down keywords they remember when you have finished the reading.
5. Read the passage again and ask them to summarise the text in one sentence. Ask three or four students to read out what they have written.
6. Read the passage a third time and tell them that after this reading they will have to reconstruct the text as fully and accurately as possible, working in pairs now.
7. Give the text to one of the students to read out very slowly so that everybody can correct what they have written. Explain that abandoned Christian churches are often bought by people to turn into homes.
8. End with a general discussion of credit cards and how they work in the students' societies.

Postscript

The words of Alice Douglas were reported by Arifa Akbar in *The Independent* newspaper on 28th September, 2006. This is a highly-abridged version of the original.

- In 2006 the average Briton had twice the debt of the average European.
- UK borrowers accounted for one third of the unsecured debt (non-mortgage debt) in Western Europe. Western Europe had a population of 300 million – Britain had a population of 60 million.
- The Citizens Advice Bureaus in the UK dealt with 1.25 million new cases of people worried about their debts.
- The average English student left university after a three- or four-year course in debt to the tune of £30,000 pounds. The universities charged each student a tuition fee of £3,000 per year.

Seven years ago, I moved to Wales and bought a church for £54,000. I thought I could do the renovation work for £80,000 but I had to spend £300,000. I did not think of the cost and used every credit card I could get. You get sucked into it and get used to spending large amounts without thinking about it, because it's on a card. It does make a difference because it doesn't feel like real money. If it did feel real, it would feel obscene.

The printed word

How much print reading do you do?

Cultural content

A comparison of students' reading habits with UK ones.

Preparation

Photocopy the **Who reads most, when and where?** table, one per student.

Procedure

1. Put these questions up on the board:
   - How much *screen* reading do you do outside work/study?
   - How many hours a week?
   - How much *print* reading do you do a week in these situations?

     in bed
     in the living room
     in the bath
     in the toilet
     while commuting
     during breaks at work
     on holiday
2. Group the students in threes and ask them to come up with their estimates.
3. Give each student the UK table and ask them what differences they would expect between people in their country and people in similar occupations in the UK.
4. Discuss the implications of all these statistics in plenary.

Postscript

There is plenty of cultural mileage in this activity. In other words, it is only *partly* about print reading habits. For example:

- A UK assumption is that a lot of people take baths, which will not be the case in a culture where showers are the norm.
- Keeping books in the toilet is not a norm in all cultures.
- If everybody commutes to work by moped, then reading while commuting will be impossible.

The survey – of 1,600 Britons – appeared in *The Independent* newspaper on 4th March, 2004. (Our version is abbreviated.)

Who reads most, when and where?

	Accountants	Secretaries	Journalists	Taxi drivers	Chefs	Teachers
Average hours spent 'print reading' a week:	5.15	4.59	4.57	4.46	4.27	4.27
Average minutes spent reading ...						
in bed	35	43	45	24	40	50
in the living room	15	19	15	10	15	14
in the bath	3	1	0	2	1	3
in the toilet	1	0	0	0	3	2
while commuting	26	18	15	0	3	1
during work breaks	1	5	0	50	10	0
on holiday	16	13	17	12	22	28

We and they

Are 'we' only a sort of 'they'?

Cultural content

Students take on board the relativity of cultural viewpoints, however polarised.

Preparation

Have copies of the Rudyard Kipling poem *We and They* ready to distribute.

Procedure

1. Dictate the first two stanzas of the poem to a volunteer scribe at the board.
2. Rub out four or five words from different parts of the text. Ask someone to read out the full text with the erased words in. Erase three or four more words. More students read the full text after each reading. Continue until there are only one or two words left in each line, and people are reading rhythmically and well, from memory.
3. Ask the students to close their eyes and relax. Tell them to notice their breathing but not to change it. In a low gentle voice, read them all four stanzas.
4. Get the students standing in a circle and lead them in an energetic choral reading of the whole poem.
5. Divide the students into four groups and get them reading chorally in canon:
   - Group A reads Stanza 1.
   - As Group A starts Stanza 2, B starts Stanza 1.
   - As Group A starts Stanza 3, and B starts Stanza 2, C starts Stanza 1, etc.
6. Now allow the students to read the poem silently, and to ask questions about words they are not sure of.
7. For homework, ask the class to use the poem as a model for writing a poem of their own about an immigrant group they feel distant from and which they guess feels distant from them. To do this effectively, the students need to find their own polarities in the middle two stanzas. Stanzas 1 and 4 need only small changes.

We and They
Rudyard Kipling

Father, Mother and Me,
Sister and Auntie say
All the people like us are We,
And everyone else is They.
And They live over the sea
While We live over the way.
But – would you believe it – They look upon We
As only a sort of They!

We eat pork and beef
With cow-horn-handled knives.
They who gobble Their rice off a leaf
Are horrified out of Their lives;
While They who live up a tree,
Feast on grubs and clay,
– Isn't it scandalous – look upon We
As a simply disgusting They!

We eat kitcheny food,
We have doors that latch.
They drink milk and blood
Under an open thatch.
We have doctors to fee.
They have wizards to pay.
And – impudent heathen! – They look upon We
As a quite impossible They!

All good people agree,
And all good people say,
All nice people like us are We
And everyone else is They.
But if you cross over the sea,
Instead of over the way,
You may end by – think of it! – looking on We
As only a sort of They!

Chapter Four
Spotlight on the UK

Your training and your syllabus may well make you feel that this is the most obviously useful chapter in *Culture in our Classrooms*. In many countries, a look at the 'Landeskunde', 'civiltà' or 'civilisation' of the US and the UK is already built into teaching materials.

This last chapter takes you beyond the traditional 'life and institutions' material you may already have in your coursebook and looks at an English-speaking country from a more anthropological standpoint. You will find activities that focus on the UK rather than other English-speaking countries – for the simple reason that the language teaching focus across Europe is mainly on aspects of the UK and on British English. Without, we hope, being chauvinists, we are of our continent and of our country!

Nice neighbours!

An Englishman's home is his castle

Cultural content

Students compare territoriality in the UK and their own home places.

Preparation

Make copies of the texts extracted from newspapers for everyone. Be ready to tell a 'neighbour territoriality' story of your own.

Procedure

1. Give out the extracts below and ask the students to read them. Give help with any of the words or ideas they don't understand, like 'semi-detached' and front gardens divided by a low fence or hedge.
2. Ask the students to write a three-sentence reaction to the three cases, working individually and developing their own thoughts without the constraints of group opinion.
3. Initiate a class discussion by asking the students to read out some of the things they've written.
4. Now tell *your* 'neighbour' story, and invite the sudents to tell *their* stories about neighbours.
5. Round off with a discussion on territoriality and on the differences between the UK reactions in the examples compared to reactions that would be typical to the students' home cultures.

Postscript

'Hedge rage' is a collocation calqued on the term 'road rage'.

Hedge couple must sell home
A couple who cut down a laurel boundary hedge will have to sell their £600,000 house to pay the costs of a three-year legal battle with their neighbours. They were landed with a £350,000 bill yesterday, after losing their case in the Court of Appeal.

Jailed for a hedge
A British couple were jailed for 14 days last August when they disobeyed a court order. This forbade them interfering with a dividing hedge. The dispute began when they cut down a fifteen-foot hedge shared with their neighbours.

Two-year dispute over hedge ends in death
A pensioner is dead and his neighbour is being questioned by the police in what appears to be the latest case of 'hedge rage'. After a heated exchange, the neighbour shot the pensioner dead. The hedge in dispute is one-foot high and divides the lawn in front of the two semi-detached houses, each owned by one of the men.

How annoying!

There's no place like home

Cultural content

What can be learnt from misrepresentation of 'other' groups.

Procedure

1. Write up the seven ways for an English person to annoy a Scot that are listed below.
2. Ask the students what you learn from these cultural 'mistakes' about both the English *and* the Scots. For example:
   - Scottish people are very proud of their distinct national identity and don't want to be subsumed into the UK culture.
   - The English consider themselves to be the bigger brother in the Scotland/Britain relationship – and a bit superior, sometimes.
3. Pair the students, and ask them to come up with a number of things that one group in their national culture could say about another group to annoy them.
4. To round off, pose these questions for discussion in plenary:
   - What beliefs lie behind this 'cultural teasing'?
   - Could it be that these annoying comments are born out of a feeling that home culture is somehow 'better' than other cultures?

Postscript

The list of misrepresentations of the Scots is taken from David Maule's *Focus on Scotland*, Macmillan, 1989.

- Use 'England' when what you mean is 'Britain' or 'the UK'.
- Use 'British' instead of 'Scottish' in speaking of people North of the Border.
- Use the word 'Scotch' to refer to people.
- Pretend never to have heard of the poet Robert Burns.
- Suggest that the UK should have one national football team instead of four.
- Talk about men wearing skirts.
- Imitate Scots accents.

A scene on a train

What strange people!

Cultural content

Students are encouraged to react in their own culturally normal ways to the things that can happen in the UK.

Preparation

Photocopy and divide up the text as shown below.

Procedure

1. Pair the students and give one half of the text to each person. Tell them to read their halves carefully. Monitor the pairs and help with key vocabulary where necessary.
2. Get them to turn their papers over and tell each other what they have read. In doing this they will work out which part of the text comes first.
3. They can now turn over their copies and put them together. Give them two minutes to jot down their reactions to the text, working alone.
4. Still in pairs, the students should now compare their reactions.
5. Open the discussion to the whole class.

Postscript

Thanks to Judy Baker, who observed the scene and told us the story.

I was on the train, waiting for it to leave. A couple came and sat across the aisle from me. She was Chinese-looking and she sat her dog on the window seat. She took the aisle seat next to it. He was well-dressed and when he spoke it was with a posh, upper-class accent. He sat opposite the woman. There was someone else asleep in the window seat on his side.

It was a minute before departure time and all the other seats in the carriage had been taken.

A tall, young, black man came down the aisle looking for a seat. He stopped and looked at the dog, which was panting and looking out of the window. The man seated noticed his look and said: *'Got a ticket?'*

The young black man pulled out his wallet and showed the couple his ticket.

There was a pause.

The woman put the dog on the floor and moved over to let the young man sit down.

Stop picking on me!

Battling the bullies

Cultural content

Comparing attitudes to bullying in the UK and attitudes to social problems in schools in other cultures.

Preparation

Copy the text below for each student.

Procedure

1. Put several copies of the text on the walls of your classroom, or even outside in the corridor.
2. Explain that the text is taken from a UK secondary school booklet which is given to every pupil.
3. Ask the students, individually, to go and read the text. Their task is to copy it exactly into their notebooks, going back and forth as much as they like. They may only *read* in front of the text: they *write* at their desks.
4. As they finish their 'running dictation', give them the text so they can clear up spelling mistakes then group them in fours to discuss these recommendations to English 14 year olds. Are the problems that schools face in *their* country the same or different?
5. Ask them to work on their own and write three recommendations a school might make to 14 year olds, about this or any social or academic problem in the school.
6. Bring the ideas together in a plenary discussion.

Postscript

Useful websites: www.bullying.co.uk; www.antibullying.net; www.childline.org.uk.

The notice below is abridged from the *Canterbury High School Sports College*, Key Stage Three Personal Planner, 2006-7.

There are three main types of bullying:

Physical	hitting, kicking, taking or hiding belongings, including money
Verbal	name-calling, teasing, insulting, writing unkind notes
Emotional	being unfriendly, excluding, tormenting, spreading rumours, nasty looks

People react differently. It is not always possible to tell if someone is hurt or upset.

- If you are being bullied, or you know that someone else is, tell us straight away and it will be dealt with.
- Not telling means the victim will continue to suffer.
- Not telling means that the bully will carry on, probably with others too.

We all have a responsibility to make sure that bullying is not allowed to continue in our school.

What strikes you in a strange culture?

A Slovene view of Southern England

Cultural content

Students write about another culture, after first reading short passages in which visitors express their views of the UK.

Preparation

Make copies of the comments opposite for the students.

Procedure

1. Give out the Slovene texts and ask the students to read them through.
2. Ask them to re-read the comments and underline any view that strikes them as *interesting*. Tell them to cross out anything they find *uninteresting*.
3. Group the students in fours to share their opinions.
4. Each student chooses a foreign place they have been, and writes half a page of comments using the Slovene passages as a model. If students have not been abroad, ask them to write about another region of their country.
5. Go round and help with language.
6. Put their texts up round the walls and allow five or ten minutes for people to read what others have written.

Postscript

The texts are snippets from *Never Tired of London, Part 2*, which appeared in the IATEFL Slovenia Newsletter 32, 2004.

Martin Robic wrote: *At least the fish shop owner did not pretend to know where Slovenia was, nor was he particularly eager to know.*

Anita Ivic wrote: *After sightseeing, we ended up in a local pub. There was a British guy there who asked us where we were from and, when we said Slovenia, he immediately placed us in Africa!*

Martin: *What I also experienced was Marks and Spencers, with their twenty sorts of sliced bread, already-made salads, organic food, as well as a full selection of Christmas foods and sweets – in October!*

What surprised me most was that everything, and I mean everything, is already packed in plastic wrapping, from meat to salad, from fruit to bread, everything is vacuum packed. I find this a bit too artificial and sterile, since there was no way I could actually choose the apples I liked, or buy a quarter of a loaf of bread.

Not to mention that three apples in London cost as much as a student's meal in a famous Mexican restaurant in Ljubljana.

Anita: *It is interesting what menus in the UK are like: all food has positive adjectives written next to it on the menu – 'delicious fish and chips', 'home-made muffins', 'lovely cottage pie', 'tasty ...' . This makes me want to try everything on the menu.*

Petra Kesmans: *I got the impression that the British tend to consider theatre-going a source of entertainment, rather than a serious institution that is reserved for intellectuals, as is mostly the case in Slovenia. Bearing this in mind, I was really taken aback by the fact that the actors of 'A Midsummer Night's Dream' sang and danced in the foyer during the interval.*

Anita: *I bought a book and had a whole dialogue of 'thank yous' with the shop assistant. Even more, he did not only say 'thank you', but he actually looked at me and smiled as if he really meant it. I had never been treated this way in Slovenia.*

The confusion of culture shock

What is going on here?

Cultural content

How disorientating, how complete and how long-lasting culture shock can be!

Preparation

Make copies of the Indian text opposite for each student.

Procedure

1. Give the text out to the students, ask them to read it through and deal with any vocabulary problems.
2. Group the students into fours: A, B, C and D – one of each in every group.
   - Ask all the As to write a three-sentence *summary* of the text.
   - Ask all the Bs to write a two-paragraph *reaction* to the text.
   - Ask all the Cs to choose ten to 15 words from the text which the *author* would regard as keywords.
   - Ask all the Ds to come up with a dozen keywords that map *their* reaction to the text.
3. When everyone is ready, group all the As (and Bs, Cs and Ds) together to compare/discuss what they have written.
4. Ask the students to go back to their original groups to compare what they wrote.
5. Elicit feedback in plenary about what your students have learned from the passage, and from each other.

Postscript

The text was written by Pittu Laungani, in *Asian Perspectives in Counselling and Psychotherapy*, Routledge, 2004.

Indian culture shock

England, to me, came as a shock. There are as many English accents are there are dialects in India, or almost. Each of them as though spoken in a different tongue, and a few, even in forked tongues. It was difficult to distinguish between levity and seriousness, between jest and truth, between praise and censure, between affection and affectation, between acceptance and rejection.

I found it exasperating not being able to read correctly their feeling and emotions on the rare occasions when they chose to express them.

In India I had been born into a particular caste and had learnt through childhood what was expected of me in a variety of social situations, which involved a mingling of castes. But with the English it was difficult to place them in their appropriate class categories; the class divisions it seemed to me were blurred and not as clearly defined as the castes were (and to a large extent still are) in India. I could not always work out what was expected of me in different situations and of different people.

What distressed me even further was that hardly any of the English friends I made (or thought I had made) showed any curiosity concerning my own cultural origins and upbringing. They avoided personal exchanges as assiduously as an orthodox Brahmin might avoid contact with an untouchable. Either they were too reticent to ask and find out, or they were totally uninterested.

In my own state of paranoia, I chose to believe the latter. How, in the name of heaven, I kept asking myself in my increasing state of despair, will I ever begin to understand them and, hopefully, befriend a few of them.

Living in a foreign country, I soon realized, was like fighting a lone battle on several fronts: the weather, the climate, the preserved and processed food, the strange customs and conventions, the patterns of day-to-day life and, of course, the people.

On target!

What goes on there?

Cultural content

Students express their thoughts, knowledge, projections and prejudices.

Preparation

Copy the list below, one for each student.

Procedure

1. Give out the list and group the students in fours.
2. Give them 20 minutes to discuss the ideas on the list. One student should act as secretary.
3. Tell the students not to worry if they have nothing to say about a particular issue. This is *not* intended as a test!
4. Get the secretaries to report, letting this lead to a general discussion where everyone contibutes.

Postscript

This activity is obviously highly suitable for working with students who are planning a visit to the target country.

After the visit, if possible, give out the list again and ask the students to work in small groups to say what has changed, in their knowledge/perceptions. Discuss as a whole-class activity.

1. The way people dress there
2. The way people drive
3. Manners and social etiquette
4. Mealtimes and food in general
5. Family life
6. The attitude towards children and teenagers
7. The behaviour of children and teenagers
8. Homes and the way they are decorated
9. The way people relate to each other in conversation
10. Different social classes
11. Television programmes
12. Religious practices
13. The atmosphere in drinking places
14. Shops (including their opening times)
15. My general feeling about being there

How I map my country

Sketching my space

Cultural content

Students find out how they internally see their home country territory and the space the target culture moves in.

Preparation

Bring in two sheets of A3 paper for each student. Also, bring a large map of the students' country/ies, a map of the target culture country and a map of Italy.

Procedure

1. Give out the A3 paper and tell the students they will have 75 seconds to do a quick drawing. (The larger-sized paper invites the students to go into more detail.)
2. Tell them to draw a map of their country using the whole of their sheet – in 75 seconds!
3. Let the students see the corresponding cartographic map/s and give them five minutes to note down differences between their map and the professional ones.

   Can they see any *reasons* for the things they have left out, put in or distorted? Show them the map of Italy and tell them some things that Italians often do:
   - They forget the northern borders.
   - They draw a vertical 'leg' instead of a diagonal one.
   - Northern Italians sometimes leave Sicily and/or Sardinia out.
4. When time is up, bring the students into a circle if you can. Each person shows their map to the group and comments on the deletions, distortions and additions.
5. Repeat the activity steps, but this time they draw a map of the target country.
6. Show the target country map – and discuss.

Postscript

Subjective map-making can reveal interesting things about how a person visualises 'territory':

- When a person from the South East of the UK draws Scotland as a vague triangle, they are making a cultural statement.
- When they omit Wales, there is a similar statement.
- Very few British people will put in the Channel Islands or the Shetlands, though 50 percent will put in the Hebrides, the Isle of Man, and the Isle of Wight.

If you are teaching in an English-speaking environment, and if the students are in homestay, suggest they do the map-drawing exercise with members of their host family. They bring the maps to the next lesson and report on what the 'natives' said about them.

Don't let me be misunderstood

The US versus the UK

Cultural content

People from the US and the UK often get things wrong, too.

Preparation

Make copies of the two dialogues for all the students.

Procedure

1. Pair the students and ask them to decide who is A and who is B. Give Dialogue 1 to the As and Dialogue 2 to the Bs.
2. Ask the students to work on their own first and read their dialogue carefully. Then ask them to write a paragraph about the US belief discernible in the dialogue and then a second paragraph about the UK belief.
3. When they have finished, ask them to read each other's dialogues and then to listen to their partner's two paragraphs analysing the beliefs of both sides.
4. Lead a general discussion as to the values involved in the two dialogues.
5. **A multicultural class** Group the students by nationalities, and ask them to discuss whether their home beliefs are like either the US ones or the British ones, or whether they are quite different, in the context of the two situations discussed.

   A monocultural class Group the students in fives, and ask them about their own culture's beliefs in the two situations.
6. Round off the activity with a report from the small groups to the whole class and a discussion.

Postscript

The two dialogues are quoted from Craig Storti's *Cross Cultural Dialogues*, Intercultural Press, 1994.

In Dialogue 1, Craig Storti is suggesting that Americans believe that work speaks for itself, while the British person (Jeremy) feels he must achieve an interpersonal link before the work can be seriously considered. In the US, *doing* is important, while in UK *who you are*, socially and professionally, is important.

In Dialogue 2 – this time between two Americans, Bill and Mary – Storti suggests that Americans expect the British to show irritation and be upset at the missed deadline. They believe that straight talk and directness are virtues. The British person believes in understatement and not revealing strong negative feelings. For him, to talk about a 'nuisance' is more than fierce enough. And thus the two sides misunderstand each other.

Dialogue 1

Marge Jeremy, why don't you try free-lancing? Selling to some publications in the US?

Jeremy I'd like that, actually. Any help you could give me would be most appreciated.

Marge Oh, you don't need me. Just put together a selection of your pieces and send them out.

Jeremy But I don't know any editors.

Marge Doesn't matter. Just send a cover letter explaining you'd like to be their man in London. Or something like that.

Jeremy Oh, I couldn't do that.

Dialogue 2

Bill How did it go with Nigel?

Mary Much better than I expected. These English are hard to figure.

Bill What happened? Did you explain everything to him?

Mary Yes, completely. I said we were very sorry but we simply weren't going to be able to meet the deadline.

Bill And?

Mary He just said 'that's a bit of a nuisance' and changed the subject.

Bill That's great!

Worlds apart?

From Japan to the UK

Cultural content

Helping students realise their own way of seeing the UK, starting from a Japanese perspective.

Procedure

1. Dictate the questions below to the class.
2. Group the students in fours. Explain that the questions you have dictated outline some Japanese behaviours and attitudes, and ask the students how similar they think the British are to the Japanese in these areas. They will draw on what they have read and seen at the movies, as well any trips they have made to the UK.
   - How many of these questions about the British can be answered in the affirmative?
   - How many of the Japanese questions can they say 'yes' to about their own cultures?
3. Tell the students to work alone and write five questions about the British from the perspective of their home culture. For example:
   - An Italian might write: Do family members eat together in Britain and stay at the table until everybody has finished?
   - A Turk might write: Do UK people treat their guests with unstinting generosity?
4. Have the students come up and fill the board with their questions as a lead-in to a plenary discussion.

- Do the British wash carefully before getting into the bath tub? Do they soak in clean warm water for half an hour each day? Do they change both all their day clothes and night clothes daily?
- Do British trains arrive on time 98% of the time?
- Do the British aim to reach perfection in everything they do?
- Do people in the UK listen three times more than they speak?
- Do British people continually seek harmony with those they speak to?
- Do the British clearly separate things they know for a fact from their own opinions?
- Is the pronoun 'we' more important to a British person than the pronoun 'I'?
- Are there people, like *burakumin* (associated with toilet cleaners and tanners), that the British regard with fear and contempt?
- Do British people look after their aging parents by taking them into their own homes?

Public notices

Do as you're told!

Cultural content

Students first explore the beliefs that lie behind UK public notices and then compare both the notices and the beliefs with those of their own cultures.

Preparation

Make enough copies of the notices for all the students. Also, cut up one or two copies, depending on the size of your class, into separate notices, so there will be enough for everybody to get one.

Procedure

1. Give just one public notice to each student.
2. Ask them to each read their sentences to themselves quietly and commit them to memory.
3. Tell them to get up and walk round the room, speaking their notices to each other, using strong, stern voices. They then sit down again.
4. Give out the complete sheets. As the students read the notices, go round helping. Make sure they understand the local cultural background to the notices.
5. Working in groups of three, they decide what the notices show about the way people think in the UK – about their beliefs.
6. Ask the students to work on their own and write down, in their own mother tongue, typical public notices from their culture.
7. When they are ready, ask them how these are different from the UK ones, and how this part of their belief system differs from the UK one.
8. Allow time for plenary discussion.

Public notices

Parking notice

FREE AT ANY TIME

NO RETURN WITHIN 40 MIN

On a stile leading to a footpath

PUBLIC RIGHT OF WAY
CLOSED

On a pier

ENTRY FREE

UNLESS FISHING

In a university college

PLEASE DO NOT
PUT YOUR CIGARETTES OUT
ON THE CARPET

PLEASE USE THE BINS PROVIDED

THANK YOU

In a toilet

NO SMOKING
IN GENTS TOILET

THIS IS DUE TO A HEALTH AND
SAFETY REGULATION

Inside an office drawer

PLEASE STOP
TAKING PENS ETC
OUT OF MY DRAWER

THANK YOU

In a toilet

LOOK

PLEASE PUT YOUR PAPER
IN THE TOILET

On a country footpath

SLOW

PUBLIC BRIDLEWAY CROSSING

GIVE WAY TO BRIDLEWAY TRAFFIC

In a toilet

PLEASE MAKE SURE
YOU TURN OFF THE LIGHTS
WHEN YOU HAVE FINISHED

On a dustbin

ONLY LOSERS DROP LITTER

In a toilet

PLEASE FLUSH AFTER USE

On a river bank

BEWARE SLIPPERY STEPS

In a garage, on a petrol pump

YOU ARE BEING RECORDED
BY SECURITY CAMERAS

MAKE SURE
YOU HAVE SUFFICIENT
FUNDS TO PAY BEFORE
YOU TAKE FUEL

Behind a campsite tap

FOR FILLING
WATER CONTAINERS ONLY

PLEASE DO NOT
DO YOUR WASHING UP HERE
OR HAVE WATER FIGHTS

WATER IS EXPENSIVE

In a petrol station

PETROLEUM SPIRIT

HIGHLY INFLAMMABLE

NO SMOKING

SWITCH OFF ENGINE

NO NAKED LIGHTS

Round a church tower clock

TRIFLE NOT

THY TIME IS SHORT

On grass

NO PARKING ON THE GRASS

PENALTY £40

On a seaside promenade

NO CYCLING

BY-LAW 7

On a seaside promenade

NO DOGS OR CYCLES

SKATES OR SKATEBOARDS

On a wall in a town

KEEP DOGS ON LEADS

CLEAN IT UP

In a National Film Theatre toilet

PLEASE BE CAREFUL

HOT WATER

Strange sounds

Even things speak differently

Cultural content

How alien the onomatopoeic words of a foreign language can feel to a learner.

Procedure

1. Write the text below up on the board, get the students to read it and then 'drill' the onomatopoeic words – you can have fun approximating to the sub-continental sounds as best you and your students can.
2. Ask the students, in groups of four, to find the equivalent words in their own languages.
3. Now ask the groups what make the following sounds:
   - *click* fingers
   - *swish* skirts/curtains
   - *clang* the sound of metal on metal
   - *clunk* the sound of wood on wood
   - *thwack* the sound of a fly swatter
   - *tweet tweet* the sound a little bird makes
   - *plop* a small stone dropping into water
4. Go round, helping the students with the English words.
5. End the activity by getting the students to comment on the feelings of the Urdu speaker.

Variation

Do a similar lesson on both the onomatopoeic words for animal noises and the verbs that evoke the sounds. For example: *woof-woof* or *bow-wow* and the verb *to bark*. Or *baa-baa* and the verb *to bleat*.

Postscript

The passage below comes from *Maps for Lost Lovers* by Nadeem Aslam, Faber and Faber, 2004.

An Urdu speaker's feelings about learning English

Practising English was hopeless. What was a person to do when even *things* in England spoke a different language than the one they did back in Pakistan?

- In England, the heart said BOOM BOOM instead of DHAK DHAK.
- A gun said BANG! instead of THAH!
- Things fell with a THUD not a DHARAM.
- Small bells said JINGLE instead of CHAAN-CHAAN.
- The trains said CHOO CHOO instead of CHUK CHUK.

Co-operative comments

I'm all ears!

Cultural content

Raising students' awareness of the co-operative nature of British English discourse and comparing it with their own.

Preparation

Be ready to tell the class a short personal anecdote.

Procedure

1. Explain that when people have listened to someone telling an anecdote as part of a general conversation, they will often prove that they have been listening attentively by adding a moral or a comment to the story. This is sometimes in the form of a proverb.
2. Say that you are going to tell the students an anecdote and that, when you finish, you want everybody to write a short 'reaction sentence', a moral or a proverb, to prove how well they have been listening.
3. Tell your anecdote and allow the students a minute's thinking and writing time.
4. The students fill the board with their sentences, so the class can choose the ones they like the best.
5. Ask an extrovert student to tell the group a personal anecdote and repeat the above steps. Then do this with a couple more people.
6. End the activity by asking students how they respond to anecdotes in their own cultures.

Postscript

Though co-operation is a general feature in any language, this is expressed very differently depending on the language that you speak. Cultural and linguistic behaviours are often inextricably intertwined. To read more about interdependence in UK English discourse, see *Cambridge Grammar of English*, by Carter and McCarthy, CUP, 2006.

Questions of attitude

What you say is who you are

Cultural content

Students are sensitised to the way British people identify themselves by what they say.

Preparation

Make a copy of the statements list opposite for each student. Also, the key below, if you will be giving it out.

Procedure

1. Hand out the statements and ask the students to read and enjoy them.
2. Put the students into groups of four or five and ask the groups to speculate about the gender and approximate age of the speakers. They must be prepared to justify their responses.
3. When everyone is ready, get them to shout out their suggestions and justifications. Some very interesting discussions may arise here, so allow plenty of time.
4. Now give out the key if you wish and allow the groups to discuss the 'answers'.
5. Round off by asking the whole class:
   - Could these statements be said by people in your cultures?
   - Why? Why not?
   - Would these statements be equally age/gender-specific?

Postscript

The statements were made by some of Gill's friends and relations.

Key

1 An adolescent male said this.
2 Adult female
3 Adult female
4 Adolescent male
5 Middle-class adult male
6 Adolescent male
7 Middle-class adult male
8 Adult male
9 Adolescent female
10 Adult female
11 Adolescent female
12 Adult female
13 Adolescent female
14 Adult female

1 *'I don't talk on my mobile phone much at all, but I'm texting all the time.'*
2 *'Having it all means doing it all.'*
3 *'My car is my haven.'*
4 *'What's the point of buying car insurance? If I have an accident, I'd rather pay the driver myself. It's cheaper, innit?'*
5 *'My life is exactly the way I want it now. We both have good jobs, a nice house, two holidays a year together and one apart when we holiday with our friends. Kids? God, I hope not! I don't want anything in my life to change.'*
6 *'There's nothing for us to do in this town!'*
7 *'Every day it's the same. Up at 5.30, onto the train at 6.15, up to London, work all day, get home, no peace till 8.30 when the little horrors are in bed, take two or three large gin-tonics. Bed by 10.30, up again by 5.30. It's a dog's life!'*
8 *'Sometimes I wish I had a garden shed of my own.'*
9 *'In the summer we all meet up on the beach and chill out all day. In the evenings we might make a fire. It's wicked.'*
10 *'I love living in England. I have a great job and can buy what I want, within reason. I've got a lovely flat, a new car, I am my own person and I can do what I like.'*
11 *'If they're my age they are dorks and if they're older, all they want to do is have sex with you and talk about themselves all day. I can't be bothered with all that.'*
12 *'I wish I felt safer in the street on my own after dark.'*
13 *'I've been criticised for my strong opinions and I wonder if this is because of my gender.'*
14 *'I wonder about my purpose in life once my kids leave home.'*

The prince and the pauper

Acting out social extremes

Cultural content

A roleplay allows students to take a wry look at stereotypical UK class behaviours and comment on their own.

Preparation

Copy a pair of role cards for each pair of students.

Procedure

1. Pair the students – one A and one B.
2. Give out the A and B role cards and leave time for the students to read theirs. Give language help where necessary. Tell them they will have three minutes for the roleplay and that *what* they speak about is entirely up to them.
3. The pairs do the roleplay.
4. Time the three minutes and then ask them to exchange role cards. Give them time to read them then ask them to do the roleplay again, the other way round.
5. Ask the students to form new pairs and repeat the steps.
6. Allow the students whole-class time to express how they felt in these different social class roles. Below are some questions you might want to ask.

Postscript

We picked up this delicious roleplay from Keith Johnson's book *Impro*, Theatre Arts Books, 1987.

- In which role did you feel more comfortable, and why?
- What made you feel uncomfortable?
- How did you feel about the other person, in role?
- Have you observed this kind of behaviour in British people on film or TV?
- Think about people in similar positions in *your* society. How do they behave?

Role card A

- You are a UK aristocrat.
- Your family has always been rich and powerful.
- It is rare for you to meet anyone socially your superior.
- You sit upright and keep you hands in your lap.
- You move hardly at all when you speak.
- You exude quiet confidence.
- You speak slowly and matter-of-factly and pick your words – the other will wait respectfully.
- The person you are talking to you is your social inferior.
- *Noblesse oblige*: you are kind to them.
- You may or may not want to speak about whatever comes up.

Role card B

- You are lower middle class.
- The person you are speaking to is an aristocrat.
- Just look how they sit – like royalty.
- You feel anxious and apprehensive.
- You lean forwards, shoulders bent.
- You sit with both feet on the ground, with your toes turned inwards, uncomfortably.
- Your breathing is shallow and quick.
- You speak fast and indistinctly.
- This is a difficult situation for you.
- You will speak about whatever comes up.

Four ways of complaining

I don't want to make a scene, but ...

Cultural content

An introduction to the four ways the middle-class English go about complaining.

Preparation

Think about the four ways the English tend to complain:

- Inner monologue
- Sideways complaint
- Apologetic complaint
- Loud, aggressive complaint

Bring to mind a time when you complained about something in a public place. For example:

- a restaurant
- a shop
- an office
- a train/plane

Prepare to tell your students a 'complaint anecdote'.

Procedure

1. Tell the students your story then group them in fives or sixes and ask them to tell the story of a complaint that they or people they know made in a public place.

2. Explain that English middle-class people are often too embarrassed to complain out loud. They think to themselves:
   - *I don't want to make a scene.*
   - *I don't want to make a fuss.*
   - *I don't want to draw attention to myself.*

   The English person will often express upset and anger in 'inner talk'.

3. Tell the students to think back to their complaint story and imagine themselves to be an inhibited English person. They don't feel able to complain *viva voce*. They imagine their inner monologue and write down a paragraph of it.

4. Explain next that an English person will often complain to someone sitting or standing near them but *not* to the person who can do something about the situation.

   Ask the students to imagine doing 'sideways' complaining in the situation they described above. They express to a partner what they'd say in that situation.

5. Explain that an English person will sometimes summon up enough courage to complain directly to someone responsible for the situation. The person will complain, but very apologetically:

   Excuse me, I'm terribly sorry, um, but, er, this soup seems to be rather, well, not very hot – a bit cold really – sorry to be such a nuisance ...

   Ask the students to go back to their complaining situation and roleplay an English person complaining, but very apologetically and indirectly.

6. Explain, finally, that the fourth English way of complaining is to do it loudly *and* indignantly. Ask the students to try complaining this way in their own situation.

7. Round off by asking the whole class:

   How does it feel to complain in the four English ways?

   The aim here is for students to air their feelings about this aspect of being a 'native of England'.

Postscript

We think that learning to *feel* situations in somehow the same ways that natives do is a central part of fully speaking the language. Kate Fox, in *Watching the English – The Hidden Rules of English Behaviour*, Hodder and Stoughton, 2004, brilliantly analyses the four ways outlined above.

Softening what you say

You might possibly ... er ... like to try this

Cultural content

Students enter the British-English mental world of 'vague self-expression'.

Preparation

Make copies of the 'softened' passage for each student.

Procedure

1. Tell the students that what they are about to write is a text spoken by a conference organiser, and then dictate the short passage opposite.
2. Now put the list of 'softeners' on the board and ask the students to work on their own and rewrite the text, including some of the phrases. Explain that as it stands, for a British person, the text feels bare and lacking in warmth. Ask them to modify it, so that it conforms to what they think might be British English patterns.
3. When they have finished, give them the possible 'softened' passage, making clear that this is one of many ways of softening, but not the only one.
4. Explain that vague language is a strong cultural-linguistic feature of the way many British people speak English. It has to do with a belief that assertion and aggression are to be avoided. The British feel that this way of speaking creates consensus.
5. Ask the students to tell you how they feel about this aspect of UK self-expression. Are softness and vagueness seen as language virtues in *their* mother tongues?
6. Put these utterances up the board and ask the students to translate them into their mother tongues:
   - *Well, she can have an orange juice or something.*
   - *We've got sixty-odd people coming later in the day.*
   - *She's sort of more or less finished with it.*
   - *See you around four-ish.*
   - *She's got loads and loads of letters after her name, and qualifications and things.*

   They may find they need to keep the vagueness, or they may need to delete it.
7. **A monocultural class** Ask the students to compare their translations in plenary.

   A multicultural class Group the students by mother tongue to compare their translations. Gather any language isolates into an 'international' group, to compare how much vagueness their languages feel fine with.

Postscript

More on this fascinating area of UK English can be found in *Cambridge Grammar of English* by Carter and McCarthy, 2006; and *Vague Language* by Joanna Channell, OUP, 1994.

Text

We don't know how many people are coming, but the room will take 200 people. It's a lecture theatre with raked seating and a podium down in the front. If more people turn up, I'm not sure what we can do about it. We can face that one when we come to it.

Softeners

well	you know	sort of	around
really	thing	approximately	erm
something like	um	up to	do we?
I mean	kind of	I guess	place
	In the region of	actually	

Softened text

Well, actually, *we don't* ***really*** *know how many people are coming,* ***do we****, but the* ***erm ...*** *room will take* ***approximately / something like / around / in the region of / up to*** *200 people. It's a* ***sort of / kind of*** *lecture theatre* ***place*** *with,* ***you know****, raked seating and a podium* ***thing*** *down in front.* ***I mean****, if more people turn up,* ***well, um,*** *I'm not sure what we can do about it.* ***I guess*** *we can face that one when we come to it.*

House rules

Ignore at your peril!

Cultural content

There are similarities and differences in household etiquette, wherever we live in the world.

Preparation

Photocopy the floor plan and the set of house rules for each student.

Procedure

1. Ask the students to draw a floor plan of their house – give out the example diagram and 'house rules' list to read.
2. Tell them to visualise coming through their *own* front door. Do they wipe their feet or take their shoes off?

   If there is something they normally do when entering their home, they should mark it with a (1) in the relevant place on their plan.
3. On a separate sheet, the students should write their own house rules.
4. When everyone is ready, get the students into small groups to share their rules and floor plans.
5. Now ask each group to come up with five *similar* and five *different* rules they have found through their conversations.
6. The students discuss the most interesting or surprising things they discovered.

Postscript

For a class going on exchange trips: they send their plans and rules to their future exchange hosts who then send their own plans and rules back. Information like this can help integrate students into the host family even before they get there, especially if they can all have an online interview first!

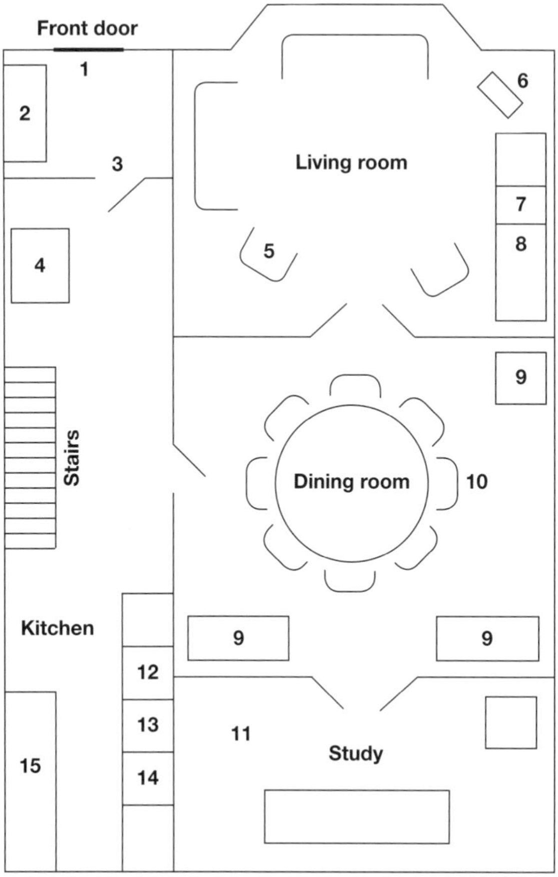

1. When you come into the house, please wipe your feet.
2. If you want, you can take off your shoes and put them here.
3. Please close the glass door in winter.
4. We usually put keys (not coats and bags!) on this table so we can find them again!
5. Dad's favourite armchair. You can sit in it, but he might ask you to move.
6. You can watch TV, but check with Mum or Dad first.
7. You can use the hi-fi, but ask first.
8. Put the CDs back when you have finished.
9. Please don't open these cupboards and drawers.
10. This is Dad's favourite dining chair, but he won't mind too much if you sit in it!
11. This is Dad's study. It's OK to go in there but only when he's there.
12. It's OK to take juice and milk from the fridge, but ask Mum if you want anything else.
13. Ask Mum about using the cooker.
14. Put your dirty plates and cutlery in the dishwasher.
15. You can make tea and coffee here.

Learning from the host family

You've got a local gold mine

Cultural content

Students think 'anthropologically' about the family they are staying with. Setting host family homework is also a way of learning language with the people they get to know best.

Preparation

What follows are ten short homework plans. Make sure you allocate sufficient lesson time:

- **Lesson 1** Enough time to set the homework task
- **Lesson 2** Plenty of time for classroom presentation and discussion

It is important to give these activities – and the students themselves – room to bloom!

Postscript

These suggestions apply to students studying in a country where English is the main language of the local people – students studying in South Africa, New Zealand, Malta, Australia, Canada or the US – as well as the UK.

Setting host family homework is a way of getting more than just language practice out of what, for many students, is a cultural gold mine – these activities also encourage the students to look at the host family they are staying with, the people they get to know best, as wonderful examples of the society they are part of. They encourage the students to think about their families in ways that go far beyond the short and entertaining activities suggested here

You might also like to adapt some of the tasks for trying with native speakers with whom the students are in contact in their home countries.

Plan 1

Lesson 1

Ask the students to tell you what image certain middle-sized towns in their countries have for them (Fuchou for a Chinese, Oulu for a Finn, Gifu for a Japanese, Zilina for a Slovak and Valdivia for a Chilean). Their image will be based on a mixture of knowledge, hearsay and prejudice – this is fine for the activity.

Pick three middle-ranking towns from the English-speaking country they are staying in and tell the students to ask their host families what image they have of these places. (In the UK we have used towns like Hull, Oxford, Swansea, Glasgow, Exeter, Sheffield, Aberdeen, etc.)

Lesson 2

The students report on the things the host families have said and compare these with their own feelings about similar-sized towns in their own countries.

Plan 2

Lesson 1

Suggest to the students that they ask the host family how many houses they have lived in, which one they liked best and for what reasons.

Lesson 2

The students pool what they have discovered about native attitudes to 'the house'.

Plan 3

Lesson 1

Prepare some of your own stories about neighbours you have had. Tell *your* 'neighbour' stories and elicit one or two from the students. Ask them to tell their own stories to the host family. Their tellings are likely to elicit host family memories of neighbours *they* have known.

Lesson 2

The students pool the neighbour stories they have elicited.

Plan 4

Lesson 1

Briefly describe to the students a person you admire (from public or private life) and then someone you hate and despise. Group the students in threes and ask them to do the same. As homework, they ask the host family for their heroes and hate figures.

Lesson 2

The students cover the board with the names of the heroes and otherwise. You call on six people to report on what they were told about their two people.

Plan 5

Lesson 1

Give the students a ten-minute lecturette on the educational system in the country they are visiting (nursery/primary/secondary/tertiary, public and private, recent debates, etc). Ask them to find out from the host families what they feel about the educational system.

Learning from the host family

Lesson 2

They report back and you ask them to take notes on the technical terms used.

Plan 6

Lesson 1

Give the students copies of some short document that is intriguing in terms of cultural values. In the UK we have used:

- the brochure of an artist who paints family groups, family pets, etc
- an advertisement from a newspaper that offers natives a course in English to help them 'speak better' and so get better jobs
- RSPCA literature (animal protection)

Ask them for their reactions. Ask them to show the document to the host family and get *their* reactions.

Lesson 2

They report back to the class.

Plan 7

Lesson 1

Prepare a list of countries that are close to the country where the students are staying or which are strongly connected to that country. In the UK we have used this list: Belgium, Holland, France, Germany, Spain, Italy, Greece, Ireland, Canada, USA, Kenya, South Africa, Australia, New Zealand, Singapore, Cyprus; and Hong Kong.

Give the list to the students and ask them to show it to the host family who pick the two countries they have had the most contact with, or about which they have the most information. The students then try to find out their views of the two countries chosen.

Lesson 2

The students report on what they have been told.

Plan 8

Lesson 1

Give out an A3, blank outline map of the country where the students are staying. They ask the family to teach them the main features of the country, marking them on the map (cities, motorways, train lines, rivers, mountains, deserts, etc). They ask the host family to tell any personal stories they associate with a given road, town or landscape.

Make clear to the students that the object of the task is not accurate information but to find out what their hosts actually know and feel about their own country.

Lesson 2

The students put their maps up on the walls so people can go round and look at them before listening to the reports.

Plan 9

Lesson 1

Ask the students which dialects or accents of their own language they can imitate. Get one or two to say a couple of sentences in their standard language – and the same sentences in dialect. Ask them which dialects of the English-speaking country they are in they can recognise. If you are able to, do a couple of dialects for them and ask for their reaction.

The homework task is to find out how the host families feel about different dialects and accents.

Lesson 2

They report on the host family attitudes.

Plan 10

Lesson 1

Give the students a 5-minute 'autobiography' of yourself as a car-user/owner. Ask them to work in threes or fours and do the same – if teenagers, they will talk about their family's car(s). Ask them to get similar car autobiographies from the host family.

Lesson 2

Kate Fox's wonderful book *Watching the English* explains how cars 'talk' – they show the attitudes and values that lie beneath our choice of car. The students can discuss what values they think are attached to the different cars the British drive and the people in each socio-economic group who drive them. They can then consider their own countries:

- Are there any cars they would need to add?
- Are there any they wouldn't want to have?
- Are the socio-economic groups the same?
- Are the values different?

Having considered cars, you might think about shoes or clothes, etc. They, too, speak volumes!

Institutions and the internet

Looking and learning together

Cultural content

Students teach each other a little about governance.

Preparation

Prepare a list like the one suggested below of the main institutional names in US and UK politics – names that are needed to follow these countries' media. You can do this activity in the computer room or set it as homework.

Procedure

1. Dictate your parallel lists.
2. Depending on the size of your class, ask each student to take responsibility for googling one or two items. Make sure all the institutions are dealt with.
3. Ask each student to pick out five salient pieces of information about each institution, and write each one down in a single sentence. No student should produce more than five sentences per institution.
4. Once the websearch is complete, draw the students together and ask them to read out their sentences to the plenary. Add information where you think it is needed.
5. Allow time for a class discussion in which the students can react to and talk about their findings.
6. Collect all the sentences and copy them for the students for the next lesson.

Postscript

This activity is a variation on an activity called 'Culture match' from the book *Cultural Awareness*, by Tomalin and Stempleski, OUP, 1994. Barry and Susan say it is an adaptation of one described by Luke Prodromou. Thank you all three!

The White House	10 Downing Street
The President	The Prime Minster
Camp David	Chequers
Congress	Parliament
The Senate	The House of Lords (legislative)
The House of Representatives	The House of Commons
The State Department	The Foreign Office
The Stars and Stripes	The Union Jack
The Pentagon	The Ministry of Defence
The Bill of Rights	The Magna Carta
The Supreme Court	The House of Lords (judicial)
West Point	Sandhurst

UK quiz

Spotlight on statistics

Cultural content

Sharing a search for some of Britain's 'vital statistics'.

Preparation

Before the lesson, copy the answers on page 88 to the quiz opposite (*without* their numbers), stick each answer onto a piece of card and distribute these around the classroom, putting them up on the walls, windows, doors, whiteboard, etc. Also, copy one quiz sheet and one answer sheet (optional – see below) for every student.

Procedure

1. Divide the class into pairs, distribute one quiz sheet per pair and ask them to read the questions carefully.
2. Deal with any comprehension difficulties in plenary and ask the students if they know or can guess any of the answers to the questions.
3. Tell them that the answers are on cards around the classroom.
    - All the students need to do now is find them.
    - The winners will be the pair to find the most correct answers – the Brains on Britain!
4. Let the activity commence!
5. When everyone is ready, either give the students the answer sheets or go through the answers with them. They can all have a complete set of questions, too.
6. For homework, ask the students to compile a similar quiz for their own countries, using the quiz sheets as a guide. This could provide further lesson activity or could be incorporated into a class magazine, for example.

Postscript

We learned this activity from Chris Price at Pilgrims, one summer.

UK quiz

Brains on Britain

1 What is the highest point in the British Isles?

2 What is the highest point in England?

3 Which is the largest lake in England and how long is it?

4 What is a loch and where is the longest one?

5 What and where is the biggest lake in Britain?

6 What, at 2 km long, is the biggest of its kind in Britain?

7 What is the area of Great Britain?

8 What are known as the Crown Dependencies?

9 a) What is the population of the UK?
b) What is the population density?

10 a) What percentage of people live in urban areas?
b) What percentage of people live in rural areas?

11 What is the percentage of ethnic groupings?
a) European
b) Other
c) What ethnic groups comprise 'other'?

12 What do these percentages refer to in terms of religion?
a) 71.6%
b) 5.4%
c) 23%

13 a) What are the major exports of the UK?
b) What are the major imports of the UK?

14 Who are the UK's major trading partners?

15 a) How many national newspapers are there in England?
b) What are their names?

16 a) What does GDP mean?
b) What is the GDP of the UK?

17 What is the 'employment type' breakdown in the UK?

18 When was the Union Jack 'adopted'?

19 Which countries do these saints symbolise?
a) St Patrick
b) St Andrew
c) St George
d) St David

20 Which figures represent:
a) the number of married couple households?
b) the number of single occupancy households?
c) the number of cohabiting households?

UK quiz

Brains on Britain – the answers

1 Ben Nevis ... 1,343 m

2 Scafell Pike ... 978 m

3 Windermere ... 16 km

4 A lake. Loch Lomond, in Scotland ... 40 km

5 Lough Neagh ... 400 sq km
In County Antrim, Northern Ireland

6 The Forth Road Bridge in Scotland

7 244,103 sq km

8 The Channel Isles and the Isle of Man

9
a) 61.4 million (2009)
b) 637 persons per sq mile

10
a) 89%
b) 11%

11
a) 94%
b) 6%
c) Indian, West Indian, Pakistani, Afghani, Iraqi, African, Bangladeshi, Arabian, Chinese, Polish, Czech, Hungarian and other East Europeans

12
a) Christian
b) Muslim, Hindu, Sikh, Jewish, Buddhist, other
c) No religion

13
a) Road vehicles, transportation equipment, industrial machinery, petroleum and petroleum products, power generating machinery
b) Road vehicles and parts, food products, textiles, yarn and fabrics, paper and paper products

14 Germany, US, France, The Netherlands, Italy, Japan

15
a) 8
b) The Daily Telegraph, The Guardian, The Times, The Independent, The Daily Mail, The Daily Mirror, The Sun, The Morning Star

16
a) Gross Domestic Product
b) $981.7 billion

17
a) 71% Services
b) 27% Industry
c) 2% Agriculture, Forestry and Fishing

18 1801

19
a) Ireland
b) Scotland
c) England
d) Wales

20
a) 8,975,623
b) 1,969,156
c) 1,602,032

Culture in our Classrooms has so far suggested a series of classroom activities to be used individually or in multiple combinations. Let us now assume a wider professional perspective in pursuit of a greater cultural and interpersonal flexibility.

In your teaching career, the rainbow of your students may change over time. New students will leave their own countries and move on, into your classrooms. In Italy, for example, teachers can have classes which include Albanians, Moroccans, Senegalese and other students from West Africa. Of course, these groups could change again in the future, following new demographic patterns.

And your own teaching career may require you to move on, to pastures and countries new. Here, then, are our questions:

- What can you do to help your *students*, who have just entered the strange and perhaps scary place which is your native country?
- What can you do to make these transitions easier for *yourselves*, working in a new environment where the rules are different?

Moving on

We would like to offer you some ideas to get to grips with new cultures, particularly from a Teacher Developmental perspective – suggesting four major skill areas that can be 'exercised'. Fundamental to all such exercises is the Rogerian precept that successful teachers will feel and show unconditional positive regard for their students. By this, we mean that they truly value the people in their classes, and show this respect even if the behaviour the students exhibit is challenging to the teacher's cultural norms. The problem here is the 'unconditional' part, usually only granted, as a matter of course, to young children by their parents. When we work with older children or adults, this is much harder to achieve. Sometimes we have found that the best thing we can do in a new cultural situation is to *stop* before we *judge*. Suspending judgement gives us the time and space to build rapport and to look at student behaviour in a less negative way – observing and listening, so we can truly hear things from *their* perspective.

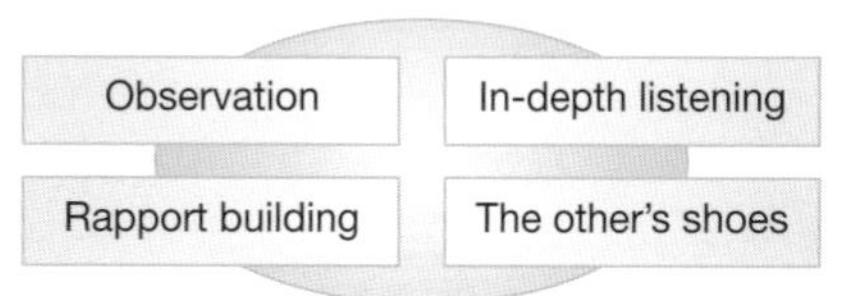

Carl Rogers was one of the founding fathers of humanistic psychology. His book *Freedom to Learn* (Prentice Hall) became a central text for many of us.

We propose 16 practical exercises, which could usefully be done in the safety of staff development sessions. Many teachers, though, do not have the support and luxury of regular Teacher Development workshops. You can, however, team up with other like-minded people – they don't even need to be teachers from your current school. What is crucial is that you all move on together.

Observation

The four exercises that follow may, at first sight, seem simple and even disingenuous. However, in our experience we have found that colleagues find it fairly hard to separate straight observation from interpretation that leads to some kind of judgement. One reason for this is that in teacher training, as many teachers have known it, 'observation' is tightly bound up with interpretation and judgement. This is why some of our colleagues find such observation very stressful and even frightening.

Let's look at an example situation viewed as straight observation and then through a cultural interpretive filter.

- Someone from one culture is talking to someone from another.
- Both are engaged in the discussion.
- Person A interjects, enthusiastically and often, while Person B is speaking.
- Person B looks increasingly uncomfortable.

An **observer** can correctly say that Person A interjects while B is speaking but that B does not interject while A is speaking. An observer might also say that B crosses his arms and legs, that he frowns on several occasions and sighs twice (ie the physical manifestations of his discomfort).

To say that *'A interrupts rudely'* is a culture-loaded **judgement**, rather than an accurate observation.

These sorts of judgements block an even-handed understanding of the situation as well as an empathetic view of the other's position.

Here are some exercises for you to try, in order to practise 'straight' observation, devoid of judgement.

'I notice'

Purpose

This exercise aims to give practice in avoiding 'second-guessing' the meaning of the actions seen. It is particularly relevant in observing a person from a different culture where our referential frame is likely to be wrong.

Procedure

- Elect one of your colleagues to tell a story (any story will do).
- Divide the group in two – half will be the 'listeners-observees' (they are going to listen to the storyteller) and half will be the 'observers'. (they are going to observe the listeners).
- Get the listeners to sit in a horseshoe around the speaker you elected.
- Allocate the observer group members a colleague to observe – and a position from which they can see their observee easily without intruding. Obviously they will need clear sight lines to do this efficiently.
- The observers take notes on what they see, throughout the delivery of the story.

We find the self-discipline of real observation a refreshing escape from vague mind-reading and guessing.

- At the end of the story, get observers and observees together in pairs. The observer will feed back to the observee, using language such as:
  - *I notice you crossed your arms five times during the story.*
  - *I notice you made a lot of eye contact with the speaker.*
- It is important that the observers do not *interpret* the behaviour; they should simply *report* it. (It is worth noting that in animal observation studies, nothing is accepted as reliable data unless observed and agreed upon by two scientists.)
- Allow time for the observees to react if they wish, then repeat the exercise, role-reversed, with a new storyteller.
- Final feedback should centre on the feelings generated by this kind of work.

Pausing

Purpose

The point of this apparently easy task is to demonstrate to the participants that observation can be crisp, clear and objective. This is particularly important in cultural contexts where a person's emotions militate against clear observation.

Procedure

- Ask two colleagues to read aloud a passage, in turn, for the group. (We suggest about ten lines from Hamlet's 'To be or not to be' speech.)
- In preparation for this, the readers will mark the text where they are going to pause, so they can be consistent – they are going to read the passage twice.
- While they read the passage, everyone else notes, in a column, the word preceding each pause made by the readers.
- The observers compare their lists and then the readers read their passage again.
- Subsequent discussion should concentrate on the importance of 'noticing what's there'. As listeners, for all the reasons listed earlier, we often fail to do this and, because of it, misunderstandings can arise.

To be, or not to be – that is the question:
Whether 'tis nobler in the mind to suffer
The slings and arrows of outrageous fortune,
Or to take arms against a sea of troubles
And, by opposing, end them. To die, to sleep
No more – and by a sleep to say we end
The heartache and the thousand natural shocks
That flesh is heir to – 'tis a consummation
Devoutly to be wish'd. To die, to sleep;
To sleep: perchance to dream. Ay, there's the rub;
Hamlet, Act 3 Scene 1

Get the picture?

Purpose

We take gestures on board unconsciously, all the time, in our interactions with people. In this exercise, we foreground the gestures and thus get a more complete, conscious awareness of the message. In terms of a culture you are meeting for the first time, the gesture system is a rich area to explore, as each culture has its own system.

Procedure

- Put your colleagues into pairs, preferably with someone they get on well with.
- One tells a short anecdote. The other listens and tries to remember all the gestures and upper-body movements that the teller produces during the narration.
- When the narration is over, the observer feeds back to the teller the gestures observed and where they occurred in the telling. Very general observations, such as 'You moved your arms a lot', are not particularly useful, as they do not link to specific moments in the text.
- When feedback is complete, the colleagues exchange roles and repeat the exercise.
- Final feedback can usefully focus on the part that gesture plays in oral communication, especially across languages.

Wildlife observers

Purpose

This task illustrates observation following total suspension of judgement. Suspension of judgement is very simple to write, but to achieve it in reality is exceptionally hard. In this exercise, it is all to easy for colleagues to wander off into 'literary style' speculation, thus abandoning observation.

Procedure

- Ask two colleagues to have a cup of tea or coffee and a quiet chat at one end of the room.
- The remaining colleagues observe the exact movements of the two interlocutors (for example: the frequency or manner of cup-lifting, changing postures, leg movements – all the movements you would expect people to make during a ten-minute conversation).
- When the time is up, the observers come together in groups of three or four to compare notes. Only movements observed by all parties can be counted as data.
- The 'chatting' colleagues circulate around the groups, to listen to the discussions; however they shouldn't *add* to them.
- Finally, the groups should bring their data to plenary.
- The 'chatters' now facilitate a feedback session and are very strict about only accepting straight description. A description such as *'leans backwards'* is fine – *'slouches grumpily forward'* is not.

In-depth listening

Normal, everyday listening is very different from the more specialised forms of listening that a human being is capable of. In normal listening we typically deal very creatively with the incoming auditory message. Sometimes we listen, not for content but for a place where we can 'leap in and say our bit'. And when we do listen for content, there are at least four ways in which we modify the incoming message – and this modification happens mostly below the threshold of awareness:

- We *delete* parts of the incoming message that do not seem relevant to us.
- We *generalise* from a cluster of detailed information so as to more easily store the ideas in mid-term memory.
- We *distort* the incoming message to make it fit better with our own pre-existing schemata.
- We *elaborate* parts of the incoming message. So, if we are listening to a story we will often elaborate the text into a kind of mind's-eye film.

In contrast, in-depth listening focuses intently on the *speaker*, on their voice quality, gestures, intonations and, as far as possible, the precise meaning they are trying to get across. The person engaged in in-depth listening does their best not to delete, generalise, distort or elaborate – staving off the tendency to do what is normal in ordinary conversational listening.

This is extremely useful when you are confronted with a cultural context that tends to raise your hackles, and the ability to switch into this mood has two effects:

- You have a better chance of understanding the message from the speaker's cultural point of view.
- The effort of 'really listening' is a powerful form of self-management, as this leaves you no time to be swept along by your own feelings.

Listening for content

Purpose

Particularly in cross-cultural situations, it is human to judge, to question and evaluate what we are being told as we listen. By forcing ourselves to block this behaviour, we create more space to listen to the actual message. When the speaker understands they have been heard accurately and wholly, this creates a much more trusting bond between speaker and listener. More cultural exchange is likely to take place under these circumstances.

The authors are fully aware that our description of the listening process is a culture-bound one and that we are speaking from within the consensus of what happens within our culture.

Procedure

- Ask your colleagues to work in pairs (A and B).
  - Person A talks to Person B for two minutes (the content chosen by the speaker).
  - Person B listens, focusing exclusively on the 'what' of the message, without judging.
  - Person B then paraphrases the content of the message back to Person A.
  - Person A gives feedback on the accuracy of the paraphrase.
- Repeat the process, roles reversed, before inviting a final general discussion.

'Musical' re-telling

Purpose

The feeling of being listened to is extraordinarily moving and satisfying, and this 'glow' affects in a positive way one's relationship with the person of the other culture. The intonation patterns and the musicality of speech do not carry the same message across different languages and cultures. Therefore the practice of listening and noticing – surrendering, if you will, to the speaker – allows for much more profound understanding of meaning within another's cultural frame.

Procedure

- Your colleagues sit facing each other in pairs.
  - Person A prepares to tell a three-minute personal story which they are willing to share with Person B.
  - Person B is asked to listen not only to the meaning of the story, but also to its musical shape.
  - The story might start slowly and with low volume, then it may pick up pace and lead to a climax and then to a quieter ending. So Person B is to pay attention to both meaning and the musical voice of the speaker.
- Person B now moves their chair round to sit behind A, to one side. They then re-tell Person A's story, using the first person pronoun as if they were A, and trying to give the same musical shape to the story as A did.
- Repeat the activity, exchanging roles.
- Bring the group back together and ask the storytellers what they felt as they listened to the re-tellings.

My distractions

Purpose

- It is very easy to become distracted as we listen – being still and receptive can be a real struggle. However, when we are distracted this can have a massive effect on the *speaker*. For example:
  - How do *you* feel when you see that your students are not 'with you'?
  - How do you feel when you are telling someone something important and you realise their attention is being 'diverted'?
- 'Distracted' listening can block you from being culturally trusted by your interlocutor.

Procedure

- Ask your colleagues to sit facing each other in pairs. Use the whole space of the room.
  - Person A speaks about a topic for three minutes (this should be timed).
  - Person B listens as carefully as possible but has pen and paper at the ready.

- Every time Person B notices a distraction in their listening, they tactfully make a cross on their paper. (There is no time to write down *what* the distraction was.)
    - Distractions can be visual (you notice a glint of light on the speaker's glasses).
    - Distractions can be auditory (your attention is caught by a distant sound).
    - Distraction can be kinaesthetic (you may have an emotional reaction to what the speaker is saying).
    - Distractions can be intellectual (you start to mentally criticise the incoming auditory text).
- After the three-minute talk, Person B looks at the crosses on their paper and tells their partner about their distractions. Person A tells Person B if these distractions affected their speaking.
- The activity is done again, with Person B as speaker.
- Come together for general feedback on the nature of focused listening and its importance in difficult cultural encounters.

Acknowledgement
We learned this activity from Mike Lavery, a business trainer in Germany.

Remembering the questions

Purpose

Remembering some of the things your students tell you is a major teaching skill, especially when you make them aware that you have remembered their thoughts, remarks and confidences. In order to make sense of behaviour from other cultures, we need to remember details which may not at the time seem important but can become significant as we 'acculturalise'.

Procedure

- Your colleagues sit in threes (A, B and C) and use the whole space available.
    - Person A offers the other two a topic they are happy to be interviewed on.
    - B and C ask them as many questions as possible about the topic for a timed two and a half minutes.
    - Person A does not answer the questions during this questioning phase. They must commit the questions to memory (no writing permitted!).
- When the two and a half minutes are up, Person A takes the time they need to answer all the questions put previously. B and C help, at the end of the process, if there are some questions that simply can't be recalled.
- The process is repeated so that both B and C can be in the 'hot seat'.
- Bring the group together for a few moments' feedback on the process and their feelings about remembering what their students tell them. Do they understand better the importance of retaining information that students offer about themselves?

Acknowledgement
This exercise is adapted from *The Confidence Book*, by Paul Davis et al, Longman, 1989.

Rapport building

Because coming into a new culture may be uncomfortable, unpleasant, even shocking, as teachers we need to be able to create good rapport with students who may be having problems adjusting to their new situation. After all, we know that we too may find situations difficult – where our own cultural norms are 'flouted'. Having good rapport with someone at these times can help negotiate these 'difficult waters' with more confidence and trust.

Maintaining deep and genuine rapport requires time and much practice. What we are suggesting here are ways of getting initial rapport that can be built upon.

We may establish rapport in a number of ways.

- Humour – when we make someone laugh, rapport is created.
- Commonality – when we establish that we have things in common with another person, this is the ground from which a relationship can grow. Here are a few examples:
  - *Place recognition.* If two people discover they both know a place, this immediately creates a bond.
  - *Intellectual.* If people discover they are enthusiastic about the same book or idea, rapport is created.
  - *Political/religious.* If people share a common political or religious belief, they will feel the rapport of group identity.
  - *Language.* If people discover they speak each other's language or if both speak a third language – linguistic rapport can even be established by demonstrating knowledge of just a few words.

Rapport is hard to define, but one way of putting it is to say that it happens when one person opens up to, and begins to trust, another.

Rapport in place

Purpose

In a staffroom where everyone knows each other well, there will be a certain artificiality in this exercise, since the room will be full of established patterns of relationships. The aim here is to give people a way of establishing rapport with someone of another culture, who they may be meeting for the first time.

Procedure

When the other person speaks the cadences of a language you know and love – you somehow love them too.

- Ask people to get up and move, to work in ever-changing pairs, trying to find a town or district (different from where they are now meeting) other parties know well. They should give some idea of the sort of relationship they have with the place:
  - Is it where their grandmother lives?
  - Is it somewhere they've been on holiday?
- They do this with as many people in the room as possible.

- Encourage your colleagues to take the opportunity to create rapport on a basis that has nothing to do with their teaching situation. This also manages to be at the same time warm, neutral and strong.
- Finally, in plenary, people should say which places created the warmest rapport for them. This exercise is particularly powerful for people who have a strong sense of space.

Rapport in listening

Purpose

When people are already in good rapport they will often unconsciously mirror each other's body position. This exercise reverses the process by an attempt to *achieve* rapport by mirroring.

Procedure

- Divide your colleagues into two equal groups, As and Bs.
    - The As prepare to speak to the Bs for two minutes.
    - The Bs leave the room and are given the following instructions: When they return to the room, they should pair up with an 'A' partner, listen to them speak and, as they listen, do the following:
        - Notice the eye-contact pattern of the speaker and replicate it.
        - Take up the same lower-body posture as the speaker. If this changes, they should change too, but discreetly.
        - Make the noises that they would normally make to show they are following the auditory text with interest. (Some English ones are: *Hmm, Aha, Wow!*)
        - Tell your female students beforehand not to physically mirror every male lower-body posture (for example: legs wide apart) if they feel awkward. Tell them to mirror the posture *mentally*.
- The Bs go back into the room, pair up with the As and do the exercise.
- They repeat the process the other way round. (It works differently now because it is more informed – there is a different quality but, also, respect.)
- Invite feedback in the pairs: How did they feel about the way they were listened to?
- The issues raised can be brought to plenary.

Proxemics roleplay

Purpose

Personal space is something so basic to our cultural identity that it is very hard to compromise upon it. However, to be aware of the problem is the first step to dealing with it in our own particular, personal way.

Rapport building

Procedure

- Ask everyone to stand up.
- Continue by working though the following steps:
  - People wander round the room, having small conversations, noticing the distance they stand apart from each other while all this is going on.
  - They repeat the process, this time taking exaggeratedly distant positions from each other, noticing the feelings this generates.
  - They repeat the process again, now standing as close to each other as they can bear within their cultural framework, noticing the feelings that arise as a consequence.
- Now divide the group into short and tall people. (If you don't know the group well, it might be best to conceal the classificatory principle!) Take the *short* people out of the room.
  - Tell them they come from a culture where it's important to come 'right up close' to have a proper conversation.
  - Tell them to go back into the room and have a 'really close' conversation with the *tall* people.
- Finally, your colleagues talk about how they felt when their sense of appropriate distance was challenged. (Often, the tall people will have retreated around the room!)
- Extend the discussion by talking about how far one can compromise, proxemically, and still remain in rapport.

Voice tempo

Purpose

Voice pacing is one of the easiest ways of getting initial rapport with a person of another culture. Amazingly, people hardly ever notice what you are doing unless they have been trained in rapport techniques – they will take it as an act of respect.

Procedure

- Divide the group in half: As and Bs.
- Take the Bs out of the room and tell them that when they go back in they will ask an A partner to choose a topic of conversation. It must be one they can both relate to. The Bs' main focus of attention should be the tempo (speed) of their partner's speech.
  - They are to adopt the same tempo as their partner, increasing or decreasing tempo as *they* do.
  - They must not tell their partner about the instructions for the exercise.
- The Bs go back into the room and do the exercise.
- Feedback should focus on how both As *and* Bs felt during the exchange. Often one or two pairs will also assume mirrored body posture naturally, showing physical rapport is in place.
- It is worth explaining to colleagues that tempo of speech and speed of thought and reading are often correlated, and that to adopt the rhythm of the other is a powerful act of respect that allows you to feel a lot closer to them.

The other's shoes

We have a Brazilian friend who, when she visits a country whose culture she does not know, spends a couple of hours discreetly imitating the way both men and women walk the streets of their town. She says that physically entering the world of body movement of the new culture programmes her unconscious to begin to willingly accept other features of that culture.

We feel that Neuro-linguistic Programming is right in helping people to go into what NLP calls 'second position' and to thus try and *live* the experience of the other. This is easier said than done – people find it hard to imagine the map of reality that the other person has in their head.

A really tough example:

- When first reading about 'suttee', or the immolation of the widow in some parts of India, we are shocked and disgusted, with no wish even to *try* and understand it from their point of view. However, when reading a text written by a 19th century widow about how she fiercely wanted to follow her husband into the life beyond and how she desired to mount the funeral pyre, we are stopped in our tracks, having to actually 'listen' and try to go into 'second position'. Trying to make internal sense of her words dents the security with which we feel that the custom of *suttee* should be seen as inhuman.

However, when dealing with a person from a culture that is strange to us, the ability to see the world, at least partially, from their point of view is of central importance. Many activities in *Culture in our Classrooms* have been about abandoning our own entrenched, or 'primitive', initial cultural perspective – enough to allow some initial understanding of a radically different cultural view.

The ability to step into someone else's shoes is so important to us – both as teachers and as students of foreign cultures. The four exercises that follow are to do with 'second positioning' in general, without any specific reference to culture. You might try them in a Teacher Development session aimed at increasing teacher sensitivity to students, but they are equally useful in inducing imaginative, cultural flexibility.

Feeling with the other

Purpose

Useful in coping with the 'cultural other' is the ability to empathise and intuit, to rely on our unconscious mind's accurate perceptions. We feel that this sort of exercise helps to develop and check out your intuitive powers.

People who have very strong ego-positions do not step lithely in the shoes of 'the other'. Many teachers have quite strong 'ego states' (or 'first positions') – after all, we are a profession of institutional leaders.

Procedure

- Ask one colleague to sit on a chair – the 'hot seat' – facing the group, and to take up any posture they please. It needs to be one they can comfortably hold.
- Ask other colleagues to come up behind them and say a sentence they think describes the feeling behind the stance. They should do this in the first person, speaking as the 'sitter'.

- After five or six people have done this, ask each of them to repeat what they said. Their colleague then chooses the sentence that is closest to what *they* might have said.
- The person whose utterance is chosen then comes and sits on a chair facing the sitter, who starts a conversation with this person, beginning with the sentence chosen. The conversation should last 45 seconds (time it).
- Repeat this sequence, with half a dozen colleagues on the hot seat.
- Round off with a general feedback session on the various emotions aroused by the exercise. Make clear that the people who came out and 'doubled' the 'hot seat' person were using their powers of empathy and intuition, the ability that Jakob Moreno, the father of psychodrama, used to call 'tele'.

Acknowledgement
This exercise comes from Linguistic Psychodramaturgy, worked on over long years by Bernard Dufeu.

Age role-reversal

Purpose

This exercise is about flexibility and the ease with which we can abandon our 'ego position', thus enabling us to take on the stance and the feeling of 'the other'. People with overly strong ego positions find accommodating to another culture quite difficult. Chameleon-like people find it much easier.

Procedure

- Bring in some photos of children, perhaps of the ages your colleagues are teaching. Ask people to get into groups of about four or five. Your colleagues should pick one picture each, preferably of a child who is not of their gender, and return to their group. Each colleague should speak as the child in the photo.
  - **Round 1:** They introduce themselves, in turn, to the group and say what's happening for them *right now*.
  - **Round 2:** They tell each other what led up to the photo being taken.
  - **Round 3:** They tell each other about their hopes and ambitions for their future.
  - **Round 4:** They are now 90 years old. They have just found the photo of when they were young and beautiful – with such dreams! How did their lives turn out? What did they actually do?
- For feedback, dictate these questions:
  - *How did I feel as the opposite gender, as a young person and as a 90 year old?*
  - *How was it, going from one role to the other?*
  - *How much of myself was invested in the role(s)?*
  - *How much do I already step into their shoes when I meet a person from another culture?*
- In plenary, you can discuss all these issues with your colleagues.

Left-hand/right-hand writing

Purpose

If you want to deal flexibly with forays into cultures you do not yet understand, then this self-management technique can be directly and practically useful. In Neuro-linguistic Programming, this attempt to be in the other's shoes and look at your own self from outside is called 'second-positioning'. In our view, developing second-position ability is central to dealing with what are to us strange and distant cultures.

Procedure

- Explain that you are going to offer your colleagues an exercise they can do in complete secrecy and that encourages them to see another person's point of view more clearly.
- Ask each person to write a dialogue between themselves and a person they are, or have been, in conflict with. They are to use their 'best writing hand' to express their own point of view, and their other hand to express the feelings of the other person.
- Tell them they have 15 minutes for the production of the dialogue. No one else will see what they have written.
- Have a ten-minute coffee or tea break and ask people to think about something else during this time.
- Give them 15 minutes to write a new dialogue between themselves and the conflict person. This time, they use the better hand to write *the other person's* side of the confrontation and their weaker hand to express *their own* thoughts.
- While the content of their dialogues must remain out of bounds, a plenary feedback session should look at how people felt, hopping again and again from one side of the fence to the other.
- Suggest to the group that this role-reversal exercise can usefully be used in situations of cultural conflict.

Acknowledgement
We learnt this technique from Bonnie Tsai.

Role-reversed letter writing

Purpose

We feel that the ability to mentally and emotionally role-reverse is central to a successful political negotiator, to a master salesperson – and to *any* expert in the area of cross-cultural work.

Procedure

- Use up all the available space, and ask each person in the group to write, on a loose sheet of clean paper, a short sentence explaining exactly how they are feeling right now. Not shorter than eight words and not longer than 16.

- Now ask them to exchange their sheet and their writing instrument with a person on the other side of the room.
- Tell each person to *copy out* the sentence they have just received, right under the original sentence.
- When they have all done this:
  - Ask if the two sentences, though identical in meaning, actually *look* the same.
  - Ask them to notice the way their partner makes letters like *h*, *f* and *m*.
  - Ask them to notice letters like *y*, *g* and *j*.
  - Ask them to notice the slope of the writing.
  - Ask them to notice the groups of letters that are joined up and the breaks.
- Now ask them, using their partner's pen but their own handwriting, to write a one-and-a-half-page letter to their partner. (The content is whatever they decide.)
- Allow enough time for each person to have got roughly halfway through this task, and then say:
  - *Stop right where you are.*
  - *Exchange pen and letter with your partner.*

    ...

  - *OK, now you have the first half of a letter from your partner to you.*
  - *Please write the second half of the letter, continuing your partner's train of thought and imitating their handwriting style.*
  - *Try to be your partner and write like them.*

  (If any of the quick ones have already finished their letter, ask their partners to write five or more PSs. This will generate enough text for the role reversal.)
- Allow time for the partners to read each other's letters and talk about the role-exchange experience, before ending with a general feedback session.

Our feeling is that the proposals in Part C of *Culture in our Classrooms*, while focusing on better and more skillful ways of dealing with people from other cultures, are also about the core skills of teaching.

- If we fail to *observe* our students, how can we mould what we teach to fit the way they are?
- If we don't offer ourselves the chance to listen to our students *in depth*, are we not passing up a fascinating learning opportunity?
- Were we to neglect *rapport building* with our students, we would make our own lives as uncomfortable as a constantly grating door.
- Perhaps the most pleasurable part of using our interpersonal intelligence is the ability to be *in another person's shoes* and enjoy our skill in seeing things, at least a little, from our students' point of view.

Our hope is that you will enjoy doing these developmental exercises with your colleagues – as much as we have enjoyed preparing them and doing them with ours.

From the editors

Culture in our Classrooms acknowledges and celebrates the role of culture in the teaching of languages. Authors Gill Johnson and Mario Rinvolucri have explored the elusive but essential notion of culture from many different angles.

They have provided a very coherent and principled set of activities which are practical, easy to implement and absolutely guaranteed to be both thought-provoking and hugely enjoyable.

- A personal perspective on culture, society and the individual.
- An examination of cultural values and behaviour.
- An explanation of cultural capital and cultural codes.
- A reflection on culture, language and language teaching.

- Cultural content – the 'what' to teach, through more than 80 activities that provide the 'how' to teach it.
- A multitude of aspects of culture – in classroom activities that promote communication and encourage critical thinking.
- Four chapters – fostering cultural awareness, focusing on the cultural connotations of language, formulating thinking frames for further study and, finally, concentrating on the UK: the 'English-speaking country' of the authors.

- Approaching culture in the context of teacher development.
- Sixteen practical exercises for staffroom sessions.
- Four strategic skills for personal and professional improvement.
- Focus on observation, listening, rapport building and empathy.

In short, we feel this is an important book that deals with an increasingly important element of the contemporary language classroom. Giving a cultural dimension to lessons is a worthwhile and immensely motivating journey – for both students and teacher.

When you opened *Culture in our Classrooms* you already took the first step.

Mike Burghall
Lindsay Clandfield

From the publisher

DELTA TEACHER DEVELOPMENT SERIES

A pioneering new series of books for English Language Teachers
with professional development in mind.

Culture in our Classrooms
by Gill Johnson and Mario Rinvolucri
ISBN 978-1-905085-21-7

The Developing Teacher
by Duncan Foord
ISBN 978-1-905085-22-4

Being Creative
by Chaz Pugliese
ISBN 978-1-905085-33-0

Teaching Unplugged
by Luke Meddings and Scott Thornbury
ISBN 978-1-905085-19-4

For details of future titles in the series,
please contact the publisher or visit the DTDS website at
www.deltapublishing.co.uk/titles/methodology/delta-teacher-development-series

---

Also from DELTA PUBLISHING

professional perspectives

A series of practical methodology books designed to provide teachers of English
with fresh insights, innovative ideas and original classroom materials.

Creating Conversation in Class
by Chris Sion
ISBN 978-0-953309-88-7

Challenging Children
by Henk van Oort
ISBN 978-1-900783-93-4

Dealing with Difficulties
by Luke Prodromou and Lindsay Clandfield
ISBN 978-1-905085-00-2

Humanising your Coursebook
by Mario Rinvolucri
ISBN 978-0-954198-60-2

Spontaneous Speaking
by David Heathfield
ISBN 978-1-900783-92-7

Talking Business in Class
by Chris Sion
ISBN 978-1-900783-64-4

The MINIMAX Teacher
by Jon Taylor
ISBN 978-0953309-89-4

The Resourceful English Teacher
by Jonathan Chandler and Mark Stone
ISBN 978-0-953309-81-8

Unlocking Self-expression through NLP
by Judith Baker and Mario Rinvolucri
ISBN 978-1-900783-88-0

Using the Mother Tongue
by Sheelagh Dellar and Mario Rinvolucri
ISBN 978-0-954198-61-9

Please contact the publisher for further details:
Tel +44 (0)1306 731770 *E-mail* info@deltapublishing.co.uk
Web www.deltapublishing.co.uk
